The Perpetual
TOURIST
in Search of a Swiss Role

Bergli Books Ltd.
Weggis and Riehen, Switzerland

The Perpetual Tourist

in Search of a Swiss Role

Cover artwork by Paul N. Bilton
Cover design and lithograph by H. Merkel AG, CH-4126 Riehen
Printed in Germany by Franz Spiegel Buch GmbH, D-89081 Ulm

ISBN 3-9520002-3-X

To, for and because of Regsi.

JULY 2nd:

We were optimistic and excited about our new life in Switzerland. But all our aspirations nearly came to a tearful end at Portsmouth in the queue for the evening ferry to cross the Channel. The mood of nervous expectation which haunts queues of car drivers and their passengers waiting for ferries, swept over us. All around, drivers were making last minute checks to their vehicles. British headlights were being taped over to prevent dazzling continental neighbours. Children bounced uncontrollably on the back seats of cars, while parents argued with each other or counted their travellers' cheques for the twentieth time.

Amid this chaotic scene, I suddenly felt moved to open the back doors of our van to get out some string. In my haste I inadvertently snapped the padlock closed as I shut the doors again, cleverly locking the ignition keys inside the back. They were the only keys we had and we were completely immobile without them.

Our mood was quickly stepped up a few notches, from excitement to blind panic, as the loudspeakers ordered drivers to take their vehicles on board the ferry.

Enquiries among our rapidly disappearing fellow travellers produced a Scotsman in the queue near us with a hacksaw. He was very keen to prove his saw on our hardened steel lock by cutting it off.

While studying the lock, I suddenly remembered that we had some spanners in the van's cab. I grabbed them and removed the metal loop which held the padlock. We had the lock off and the keys out just in time to board the ferry, along with one disappointed Scotsman and his unused hacksaw.

JULY 3rd:

It was a bright Monday morning and we were among the first five vehicles off the ferry at Le Havre at 7 am. We braced ourselves for an early morning brush with the French customs, only to be waved nonchalantly through the barrier without so much as a "hany sing to declare?" Our aim was the Swiss border by five that evening.

There are many ways of getting all one's worldly goods from Hampshire to Switzerland. Unfortunately all the ones that involve a short jet flight and staying in first class hotels, while some sucker does all the packing and shifting, also involve large amounts of money. Thus we opted for the VHF method ('van hire and friend'). This is really a 'once-in-a-lifetime' method as it is hard on all concerned, even the furniture and certainly the friend.

The journey through France was long, slow and uncomfortable. The van had been booked some days in advance so that the insurance could be arranged. I had to tell the hire company the size of vehicle we required. My prediction of seventeen cubic metres was not far off the mark and all our things fitted snugly into the back of the twenty-cubic-metre Mercedes Luton van. What I had not been asked for, was the weight. It is surprising how heavy seventeen cubic metres of beds, tables, chairs, books, etc. can be. Once filled, the van took on a strange lethargic sway. Bends had to be treated with the greatest of respect as we creaked and rolled our way in the direction of Switzerland, as if in slow motion.

As the day wore on, it became apparent that we were not going to reach the Swiss border at Basel before 5.30 pm, when it is closed to commercial traffic, which included us.

When we arrived at the border it was 9.15 pm, but we decided to have a go at crossing anyway. After some debate with customs officers, we were allowed into the land of real and paper mountains, but only after they had secured the rear door lock with a lead seal. With a handful of suitably official-looking papers and minus a deposit of Sfr 100, our welcome was complete. We could get the deposit back next morning in Zurich at the bonded warehouse.

We eventually arrived at my in-laws' house in Zurich at 00.15. (Notice how I've now switched to the 24-hour clock?) I shall refer to my wife as Regula. Why? you ask. Because that is her name. She was named after a Zurich saint and martyr who, along with a certain Felix and Exuperantius, had her head cut off by the Romans when they were in town. Ever since the good citizens of Zurich have often called their daughters Regula, their sons Felix and those they are unsure of, but nevertheless hopeful for, Exuperantius.

Regula's parents were pleased to see us and our friend Mark, who immediately disgraced himself by asking if the Zurich water was fit to drink.

JULY 4th:
There is no respite for us. The van and Mark are booked on the ferry back

from Le Havre with a 60 hour, cheap (or rather less expensive) return ticket. We were up early at 6.30 to go down to the bonded warehouse in Zurich to have the seal removed from the van and this time be properly welcomed to Switzerland.

This was my hope. We did much the same in reverse seven years ago, when we moved the contents of Regula's Zurich flat to England. That time the van was smaller, lighter and faster. Then, just as we have done now, we carefully listed everything we had with us. On our arrival at Southampton, we waited with some trepidation in the red, something to declare, customs lane. I explained to the British customs officer that we were transporting all my fiancé's things over to England as we hoped to marry shortly. The officer did not even glance at our list or what we had in the van. Instead he beamed at us and with a cheery wave sent us on our way, but not before he had congratulated us on our forthcoming wedding.

The Swiss customs did not look in the back of the van either, but that is where the similarity ended. Maybe if I had had the right paperwork our Swiss welcome would have been warmer. But I didn't and it wasn't.

We were stuck at the bonded warehouse for over an hour because I had no entry permit. I had applied for one two months before from the *Fremden-polizei*, the 'foreign police', which is a strange name because they are Swiss and not foreign at all. They are the Swiss equivalent of Mr. Orwell's thought police, who deal with such things as entry permits. The customs man, who combed his hair forwards from the back of his head to cover his bald patch and occasionally cleared his throat in a disgusting manner, decided that as nearly everything else was in order he would get us on this. Furthermore, instead of returning our hundred francs, he decided that it was not enough and he would like us to leave more of our money in his care.

I pointed out, via the translation services of my wife, that I felt this permit had little or nothing to do with customs and anyway we had already entered the country, permit or no permit. Wasn't he more interested in the van load of heroin we had outside his window? I suggested that he phone the thought police himself and see what they had to say about the entry permit.

Regula omitted the bit about the heroin and our customs man was so taken with the idea of phoning that he did it at once.

Some things are very similar wherever you are in the world and one of them is trying to get information from a government office by phone. It is not that they will not give you the information, it is simply that when you eventually get through, having got the engaged tone the first few times, they always refer you to another number. This system also applies in Switzerland. After being given three numbers (the third one was obviously the right one as it was permanently engaged), our customs man found he had spent more than the required time on us for the value of goods we were carrying, and moreover, his coffee break was about due. He hung up the phone, primed his rubber stamp and

carefully thumped every piece of paper we had. He then went out with us to the van, removed the seal and clipped it to his copy of the paperwork, gave us our Sfr 100 back and disappeared for his coffee.

We were on our way again and nobody had opened the back since I locked the keys in at Portsmouth. Bearing in mind that the van can be opened with a spanner, seal or no seal, it made a bit of a mockery of the whole process.

We arrived at our flat later than intended, got the door keys and started unloading. By 8 pm we were finished (in every sense). We pushed one or two boxes around and made up three beds.

JULY 5th:

We fed Mark an early breakfast and sent him and the van on their way back to Blighty's shores. As the large red words 'Ringwood Van Hire' disappeared round the corner at the end of the road into the morning traffic, I realised that there was no going back. I have cut my ties with the land that has been my home for the last forty years. A very poignant moment, but there was so much to do that I did not have time to ponder further.

JULY 10th:

Still up to our necks in unopened boxes.

What is an Englishman with no Swiss apprenticeship or qualifications to do in Zurich? In England I had worked in advertising and publishing and I had extensive experience of running a small business. But I cannot speak German. A year at night school in England extended my vocabulary beyond *zwei Bier, bitte* (two beers, please), but not far beyond. I have basically two career choices in Switzerland: I could dig holes in the road, or teach English. To dig holes in the road I would need a smattering of Italian, Turkish, Serbo-Croat and German.

I decided teaching English was easier. The means to this end are not difficult, provided you are 'an educated native English speaker' who knows the Queen's English (and Prince Philip's Greek). I took a month's full-time course earlier this year in England and came away with a Royal Society of the Arts 'Certificate for Teaching English as a Foreign Language'.

My first attempt at landing a teaching job has not been a resounding success. Following up an advertisement I had been sent when still in England, I arranged a meeting with a Scotsman here in Zurich who was looking for English teachers. He had already filled the job, but he is always on the lookout for more teachers, and with good reason. He was from Scotland, but his hours were definitely Swiss.

He and his teachers work nine hours a day in three sessions – 7 to 10 am, 11 am to 2 pm and 4 to 7 pm – five days a week. He is always on the lookout for a fresh supply of experienced (and masochistic) teachers who can cope with those hours. He also wanted suckers to teach in Zurich, Zug and Winterthur, sometimes all in the same day, travelling between sessions (up to 150 km per day). He was an unbearable dickie-know-all and told me that I should always wear a tie in Switzerland. If this is what happens when you teach, maybe digging holes would be better after all.

This has not completely put me off the idea of teaching, I just feel that perhaps I should start at the shallow end. Tomorrow I am going to put on my best suit and tie then, armed with a list of language schools in Zurich, I will knock on their doors.

JULY 11th:

The first school I went to was closed. Then at the next two the directors were on holiday and I was just given forms to fill in. So I have decided to give up cold calling and I will blitz the schools with a letter and c.v. so that they will have something to read when they get back from their holidays. I have also put cards in local supermarkets to advertise private lessons at my home.

I have discovered the hard way that Switzerland, like most continental countries, closes down for the summer.

There are five flats in our building, but we have found that we will be the only ones at home for most of July. We have to lock the building at night and I was given instruction on how to use the boiler, fuses etc. in case of breakdown. Everyone else is on holiday.

JULY 16th:

These first two weeks in Zurich have been among the most frustrating in our lives. It was bad enough getting all the contents of our four-bedroom British house and garage into the van. Now, Regula and I have had to spend every waking hour trying to fit it all into a three room Swiss flat. This is how the Swiss measure their homes: it is assumed that all flats and houses have a kitchen and bathroom so these are not counted, just the remaining rooms. The British hold the number of bedrooms to be of the highest importance when assessing a property, regardless of whether there is a bathroom or kitchen at all.

Every morning we wake up early with the intention that today will be the day to clear the last of the cardboard boxes away. At midnight we collapse into bed exhausted, still surrounded by half-unpacked boxes. Ironically we had to borrow Regula's father's car to go and buy more furniture, a book shelf to accommodate all the books, photos and rubbish we brought with us. We should have been much more ruthless and thrown more things out back in England.

The weather has been hot and muggy since we arrived. Swiss summers are generally hotter, sunnier and wetter than English ones. The rain tends to come in heavy thunderstorms, often at night. Certainly we notice that Switzerland is very much greener and lusher than England, which, according to the news, has been experiencing a heat wave since we left. Very unfair.

JULY 17th:

At last we have managed to force some kind of order upon our possessions. And just in time too, because today Regula starts her job that she had arranged earlier from England.

In the meantime I am becoming a *Hausmann*. I never did much shopping in England, so I cannot compare commodities too well. I am trying desperately to think in Swiss francs (Sfr), as converting to pounds is making me feel ill. I have found it easiest to convert at ten francs to the pound. This has the advantage of being very easy to calculate and, although totally inaccurate, is far less distressing.

Regula optimistically reckoned that the Swiss shopping bill should be only a little higher – a few things cheaper, a few more expensive (but all much nicer in Switzerland she says). The reality is that prices are generally 50% more than in the UK and anything that involves labour is unbelievably expensive.

For example, the Müllers, who are our landlords (not the Mullahs from Iran), had asked us if we would like the police to put a 'no parking' sign outside when we unloaded the van. We said "yes please". Of course it was done perfectly and a little no parking sign was there to greet us when we arrived.

However, we were then presented with a bill for Sfr 35 from the police for bringing and taking away the sign.

There is one bargain though, and that is public transport. We each have a 'Rainbow Card', a monthly ticket for the whole of the town of Zurich which entitles us to unlimited use of the trams, buses and trolley buses. It pays for itself within a week compared to buying single tickets, and it is so convenient to just jump on a tram and pop into the centre of town, only a twelve-minute ride away.

The other day I was on a tram and a boy about twelve, on his way home from school, was drinking a McDonald's milk shake when the tram made an emergency stop at roadworks which are the curse of Zurich. The whole place is continuously being dug up. The milk shake went flying across the tram floor and made a filthy chocolate puddle. An old lady on the tram said he should clean it up and lo and behold he took out his swimming towel and did just that. At the next stop he hopped out and put the carton in a bin. I very much doubt a schoolboy would have cleared up such a mess on a bus or train in England.

JULY 24th:

I have discovered that the thing to do with Swiss prices is simply not to convert them into pounds. Otherwise it makes my hair curl. I now always think in terms of how long one has to work to pay for something, and that comes out much more favourably. If I taught English in England I would have to work for seventeen minutes to buy a bottle of plonk, here I would hardly have started and after a mere three minutes I could, theoretically, nip out and buy a bottle. All I need now is that teaching job.

Regula seems to have enjoyed her first week working for a lawyer (solicitor) who has more money than he knows what to do with. This is the first time for seven years that she has worked full-time. She had a number of temporary jobs in England, but they did not live up to her qualifications. She is a secretary. In Britain this may not carry much weight, but the Swiss are great believers in training, qualifications and education. To be a secretary she had to study bookkeeping, business administration and even a little commercial law, among other things, as well as typing. Of course she speaks German, English and French. These skills were not needed, nor paid for in Britain. In Zurich she is able to command a salary three times the amount she could get in England.

The Swiss work longer hours than the British and thus at least give the appearance of working harder. We get up at 5.45 am each morning so Regula can leave at 7.10 to start at 7.30. This is a little earlier than most offices here, but by no means unheard of. For example this morning we had some mineral water and beer delivered. (These are naturally only supplied in environmentally friendly returnable glass bottles with a deposit.) They are very heavy to carry from the supermarket, not to mention returning the empties back again. The delivery man arrived at 7.30 am. Food shops open at 7.30 or 8 am, but I have to watch lunchtime closing – often this is 12.30 to 2 or even 2.30, but all shops are open until 6.30 pm.

Since Regula starts so early, she finishes at 4.30 pm. It sounds like a good job. All the staff at the lawyer's office have personal computers on their desks and they can all stop to eat croissants, butter and jam supplied by the company at their coffee break. The coffee is, of course, expresso and it is available all day from a machine that grinds the beans and then brews the coffee to the highest Swiss standards. This would be wonderful, but apparently there is no time to sit around and drink it.

JULY 25th:

In expectation of future financial improvement, I have opened a bank account. The funny thing is nobody uses cheques in Switzerland, except Eurocheques and travellers' cheques. Bills are submitted by tradesmen, telephone, electricity etc. for payment at the end of the month. With the bill they supply a paying-in slip giving details of their postal giro account. I use these to instruct the bank with one order to pay all the bills, rather like credit transfer in the UK but without writing a cheque. Cash is the main means of payment.

This can lead to some odd problems: we qualified for a refund on a bill and the postman appeared on the doorstep with the refund in cash. As always, he contrives to call when we are out. He left a little note telling us to call at the post office personally. Thus with passport in hand as identification, I had to queue at the post office to collect the refund, which was, as always, less than anticipated, and the queue I picked was the slowest. I cannot help thinking that cheques must be easier.

Credit cards are tolerated, mainly to keep tourists happy. Bancomat automatic cash dispensers are everywhere, except when you really need one. Current accounts pay a modest interest (when there is some money in them) and bank charges are low.

When you open an account you can nominate which language you would like all communication to be in. Everything I get from the bank is in English. They also sent me a very elaborate brochure in English with floor plans of my branch explaining where all the facilities are. I can watch videotext while withdrawing cash, then put the cash into another machine which changes the notes to coins. If these are still too big, I can change the coins to even smaller ones still. There are also two Changeomats that convert Swiss Francs to foreign currency and visa versa. There is a Goldomat for buying gold and gold coins. There are TV screens with American news all day long from CNN (Cable News Network). The whole building is based on the design of the bridge of the Starship Enterprise. The only thing is, there do not appear to be any toilets.

JULY 27th:

On the recurring subject of officialdom and paperwork, we have encountered more difficulties. It was our understanding, and Regula was so advised when she enquired from England, that as I am married to a Swiss national, I do not need a work permit. This is not true.

Whilst everything in Switzerland is methodically and logically supported by rules, regulations and paperwork, these can vary widely depending upon where you live. The rule in one valley is not always the rule in the next. Recent changes have helped to cloud the picture further. Originally if a Swiss man married a lady of foreign origin, she automatically became Swiss. But a Swiss lady marrying a foreign man not only could not bestow Swiss citizenship upon her new partner, but even stood in grave danger of actually losing her own Swiss nationality. This was obviously unfair, so the wheels of equality turned in their slow Swiss way and made both men and women equal: now neither can automatically give Swiss citizenship to their partners.

We paid a visit to Zurich's 'thought police' (the foreign police who aren't foreign). We went to shake the tree down there and see what would fall out, in particular an entry permit for me, the absence of which caused such consternation to the customs officer. They advised that it was being processed and would be sent "next week". All who live in Switzerland have to register at their local community office and likewise un-register there when they move or die, whichever comes first. Registration has to be within eight days of arrival and entry permits are required. We have already asked for, and been granted, an extension to await the thought police's thoughts.

AUGUST 1st:

August always starts with a bang in Switzerland, quite literally, as August 1st is Swiss National Day and traditionally involves letting off millions of francs' worth of fireworks. It is the day that, about seven hundred years ago, the original three cantons (like counties in the UK, or states in America) got together to swear that they would only be ruled over by a fellow countryman and not by some foreigner. And so it has remained ever since. Thus the Swiss attitude to foreigners is fairly deep rooted. Over the centuries other neighbouring groups liked the look of this federation and, having proved they were up to it, were allowed to join. Today's Swiss Federation, or 'Confœderatio Helvetica', was established in 1848 and is symbolized by a lady called Helvetia. Sadly now the Federation is full and no one else can join.

Funny word isn't it 'Helvetia'? It is simply another word for Switzerland, as I discovered as a lad when I pursued the hobby of stamp collecting for about two weeks. During that time I filled my little album with stamps from the four corners of the globe. But oddly I found that the pages for Switzerland were completely empty and at the same time I collected a large pile of stamps bearing the name 'Helvetia'. Shortly before I gave up the hobby for more adventurous pursuits, I put two and two together and stuffed all the loose Helvetia stamps in the Switzerland pages.

So if you have ever wondered why Swiss cars so illogically bear the nationality plate CH it is not so much that Sweden got in there first with S, or even Swaziland with SW, it is simply that CH stands for 'Confœderatio Helvetica'. Just as if Grand Bahama had taken GB first, Britain could have always resorted to UK.

AUGUST 3rd:

Having found that all language school bosses are on holiday until mid August I went to some job agencies to see what other work I could do in the meantime. Unfortunately all they were interested in was whether I had a work permit. I went through the usual story about not requiring one. They were unimpressed. They said they had never heard anything like it before. They thought I had it all wrong and they were not going to waste their time finding out what the position was on my behalf.

As Regula works for the boss of one of the most expensive legal practices in Zurich, she decided to put them on the case (all free of charge of course). To our amazement they were unable to give an answer straight off. They asked for all previous correspondence with the authorities and it took a Doctor 'somebody or other' nearly a day of phoning around to clarify the situation. He advised that the regulations vary from area to area and community to community. This we already knew and they probably vary from street to street too.

The conclusion is that I *do* need a work permit. But it is merely a formality and is "guaranteed". However, one cannot get a work permit until one has a job. So I have to assure potential employers that this is easy for me to obtain. To complicate work matters further, I cannot apply for a work permit until we have the confirmation from our local *Kreisbüro* (Zurich's name for the area, or community, office) that they have received Regula's papers from her *Heimatort*, this is equivalent to her home town. She is registered in a little town called Aeschi (pronounced: 'ashey') in Canton Solothurn. Not that she knows the place though, she has been there once many years ago and I do not even know where it is. It was her first husband's home town and became her *Heimatort* too when she married him. She will change it back to Zurich in due course, but this takes time and, like everything else in Switzerland, costs money. The lady in Aeschi that deals with such matters is, you might have guessed it, on holiday. So we await her return, no doubt from some tropical clime, before we can proceed further.

I am rapidly getting the feeling that Switzerland is not unlike an exclusive members-only club. There is a nice big fat cake that can only be split so many ways and keeping foreigners at bay is one way of keeping more cream for themselves. So it appears that until the right people come back from their holidays, I am unable to pursue the subject of employment.

AUGUST 8th:
The "next week" promised by the thought police for my permit has come and gone and no permit arrived. So Regula phoned them and they decided that if I was already in the country, I did not need an entry permit. Seems logical. So I went to the *Kreisbüro* myself (yes, of course, they speak English) and filled in a long form which required such unlikely information as my mother's maiden name. I was attended to by a young girl with hair heavily gelled so that it all pointed up to the ceiling giving the impression of her being constantly shocked. She looked hardly old enough to have left school, let alone deal with such life and death matters as permits and permissions. I casually asked about work permits, saying that I was of the opinion I did not need one. This produced lots of sucking in of air and shaking of heads with pointed hair. The problem was passed on to superiors. In the meantime they charged me Sfr 15 for putting a little stamp in my passport.

They also required two copies of our British marriage certificate. The girl spent a long time checking the copies with the original which like all British documents tells one nothing, no nationality, no age, even the date was a poor rubber stamp barely legible. Anyway she did her best with the poor show that Bournemouth Register Office had produced. She said if I paid a further Sfr 15, I could register for Regula too, so I did. And then almost in passing she said as I was going: "If you want to work, you must show your passport and wedding certificate."

At least now I have the OK to be here and permission to waft my marriage certificate and passport under the noses of potential employers. That should impress them all right. At least I did not have to have a chest X-ray and full physical check-up at my own expense, which is what was required when a colleague from England moved recently to the nearby town of Winterthur. (Same canton, but a different valley.) Everyone else I have spoken to in the same position has had similar experiences and got very conflicting and confusing information.

AUGUST 9th:

My passport and marriage certificate, being both British documents, are regarded with deep suspicion. I have now received a very nice little A5 size 'Family Book' with gold-leaf embossed red leatherette cover for Sfr 19 (in cash handed over to the postman). The book contains my name, place and date of birth, parents' name and, as is the custom, the maiden name of my mother. Being the husband my details come first, then Regula's. Our family book was issued by that Aeschi place, Regula's *Heimatort* or home town. This modest document is held in far higher esteem than anything that originated in the UK and is photocopied with great enthusiasm by potential employers.

In England we lived, like nearly 80% of the population, in our own house. In Switzerland the property market is very different. As a mere British citizen, I cannot buy anything even if I could afford it. Property is only allowed to be purchased by Swiss nationals or foreigners who have had permanent residency in Switzerland for over ten years, with possible exceptions for rich film stars.

Prices are at Mayfair levels, not just in the centre of Zurich, but right to the Swiss borders in all directions. Some of this is due to the style and quality of Swiss building. If you were to throw up a British style, timber-framed mock Tudor estate, no one would be interested, nor would you be allowed to build it. Houses and flats are built like tanks to withstand the severest winter conditions, not to mention a nuclear blast. The bomb would probably whip away everything above ground, but the Swiss would be cosily tucked up in what they euphemistically call their 'air protection cellars'. That means nuclear-proof cellars to you and me.

These costly building requirements and triple-glazed windows put a bob or two onto property prices. How can the Swiss afford it? They can't. Most people cannot buy, they rent. This is in complete contradiction to the British system where we are encouraged to buy. The Swiss always grumble about the price of accommodation, but they seem to be able to pay it and still afford holidays to exotic destinations each year. But while the UK property market is flagging, in Switzerland there have even been demonstrations in the streets protesting about the lack of flats available for rent.

AUGUST 10th:

Taking a break from the mounting confusion over my papers, I went windsurfing for the day with my brother-in-law, Andreas. Windsurfing is a sport that had me very confused for a number of years. Living near the south coast of England, I would see a near continuous stream of cars with boards on their roofs heading for the coast on windy days. The muckier the weather, the more these fanatics seemed to like it. I had always enjoyed dingy sailing and had owned and sailed a few over the years, but I could never get on with windsurfing. Every time I tried it, I spent the whole time falling in and getting tired, wet and frustrated.

Then we went on a holiday to the Mediterranean one summer and windsurfing was included free of charge. So I decided to get to the bottom of this business once and for all. I persevered and even made a little progress. By the second week we were shown how to use the harness. Now I never knew that there was such a thing, but there is. You put on what appears to be an oversized and rather gaudy nappy, with a large hook at the front. This hook then attaches to a loop of rope on the boom. The idea is that, with enough wind and the right balance, your arms need not be wrenched out of their sockets, but you can instead sit back and let the harness take the strain.

After many false starts and being thrown head over heels forward or sinking ignominiously backwards into the water, I finally got the hang of it. I can still remember the moment. It was a moderately windy afternoon and I caught the wind and hooked in. For the very first time I was skimming on the water like a water skier with no boat. I could feel the power of the wind, not trying to rip my arms off, but tamed through the harness. It was so exhilarating, I understood then and there what those loonies were up to on windy weekends in the British winter.

Windsurfing Swiss style was helped by a wonderful day – hot and sunny.

Wind can be a problem in Switzerland, or rather the lack of it. So we went to a lake in central Switzerland, the Urnersee. This lake has spectacular sheer cliffs at its sides and narrows at the end, so that the wind is funnelled down it. It was a fantastic new experience, skimming over warm turquoise water and looking up to snow-capped mountains towering above. Despite being glacier fed, the water is warmed by the sun so that the top metre reaches a comfortable 23° C. Being a lake, it was not so rough as the open sea would have been with the same wind force (3-4).

Unfortunately unless we get a car of our own to carry my board on, I can only go windsurfing with Andreas. A car is such an expense and we really do not need one, except for getting out at the weekends.

AUGUST 14th:

I have joined an intensive High German language course to try and extend my command of the language, which is barely higher than non-existent. I have, of course, a number of good excuses for my inadequacy in German. During the years I was at school in the late fifties and into the sixties, German was not taught at school. We British are often scorned for being monoglot, but this really is unfair. English is the most powerful language on earth. Sadly this is because it is the language the Americans use, and not through our own doing.

The Swiss find it hard to realise that you can live your whole three score years and ten in Britain and never hear another language. The Swiss wrestle with four languages of their own, German, French, Italian and Romansh. Every Swiss child who gazes at the corn flakes packet at breakfast is treated to the ingredients in three languages. The Swiss top-forty record chart is broadly the same as in the UK or America. Every hit is either American or English and there are even English DJs on Swiss radio to play them. We can watch three English-speaking channels on the cable TV system here. I could go on.

Now add to this that in the German part of Switzerland, they do not speak German at all. All right, they **can**, but the local native language, Swiss-German, is often not even understood by Germans. Swiss-German is an old guttural farmers' tongue that has managed to hold on into the twentieth century. In fact the advent of TV and local radio has actually given a boost to the language. The general rise in nationalism and the Swiss determination not to be German means Swiss-German is alive and well and living in its various forms across the mis-named German-speaking part of Switzerland. It is a language that has far less of the grammatical forms associated with High German and, to finally confuse you, it is only written phonetically and is not the same in any two towns. That's *Schwizerdütsch*! (Swiss-German.) Or is it *Schwiizertüütsch?* Or even *Schwyzertütsch*??

Among the first things children do here when they eventually get round to starting school at about six or seven years old, is to learn High German. So while all can speak it, many rarely do. The problem is though, that when they do speak High German they are expected to be grammatically perfect and not everyone is. What language are they allowed to make a complete mess in and nobody complains? Why, English of course. Those who are better at languages and do not need to disguise their weak High German love the opportunity to practice their English. So you can see that it is an uphill struggle for me to find any motivation to learn German.

Bearing in mind this background, it has taken me over a month in Switzerland to realise that Swiss-German, although spoken by the majority here, is far too specialised and localised to be of long-term good to me. We have an English friend whose mother is Swiss. When a child, this friend was caught by the outbreak of the Second World War in Grindelwald, where he had gone for a holiday at his grandmother's. He spent the duration of the War there and in 1945, at age fourteen, he went back to England. On his return he needed coaching in English, as he had spoken only *Grindelwalddütsch* for six years. He is now the only British bank manager who is fluent in both English and a dialect of a small part of the Bernese Oberland as spoken between 1939 and 1945.

It took a me a while to realise that I would not simply just wake up one morning and be able to speak another language. This is not such a daft idea as it sounds. After all, I learned English by just sort of hanging around. But that was when I was a child, it apparently does not work for adults. I am having to start learning German the hard way.

AUGUST 15th:

Here's a useful tip: if you are thinking of moving to Switzerland, make sure you are married to someone Swiss and don't turn up in July or August – the country is shut down for holidays.

AUGUST 16th:

My wife is now into the swing of her job, although the early starts are getting to us a bit. She says it is great to be able to say her name, Regula, only once and have people know it immediately. In England she seriously considered calling herself 'Susan' or 'Jane' because it got so embarrassing repeating 'Regula' four or five times every time anyone asked. That's the good news. The bad news is that now she has to repeat 'Bilton' about four or five times. The problem is compounded because in England she used her Christian name in the office and in Switzerland surnames are used much more. No one here has heard of the name Bilton. We shall be the only Biltons in the phone book when it is next published.

Regula's boss, not content to shower his staff with croissants and fruit juice, expresso coffee etc. closed up shop one afternoon and took all the staff on a 'company walk' somewhere up in the hills above Zurich. They all took their walking shoes and waterproofs to the office and did a morning's work. After lunch, which in Switzerland means about midday, they set out on a two-hour walk followed by sandwiches and wine. After a bit more walking and further eating, Regula came rolling home on the last tram only to get up at 5.45 am the next day for another day's work. The company apparently does this twice a year.

AUGUST 18th:

The job situation seems to be opening up a little for me, although the red tape continues. I wrote to a dozen language schools listed in the telephone directory. Most replied saying either the person I want is on holiday, or they have no vacancy at the moment.

I went for an interview with the Migros Club School. Migros is a well-respected and large Swiss institution, with at least one supermarket in every town and village. They have a chain of banks, an insurance company, travel agencies, petrol stations and, of course, language schools. Not unlike Marks & Sparks, but much more diverse. The woman who interviewed me said I needed to speak some German as they wanted a teacher for beginners. Like a fool I said that was no problem. So she conducted the rest of the interview in German. I nodded a bit and said *"Ja!"* every so often and when there was a gap said *"natürlich,"* nodded and shook my head as I thought appropriate and generally tried to look intelligent. However, after she had explained the wonders of the Migros outfit for about half an hour, I deduced that they wanted a teacher for just four hours a week, all on Thursday evenings.

There is a danger that my work permit, if I ever see it, could be used up on this one job. They made it clear that they cannot do anything until I have the right papers. Their facilities are very impressive and make the night schools I have seen in Britain look positively Victorian. Their classes of fifteen are seated in a large circle at specially designed director-style tables with a circular loudspeaker in the middle on a stand. This links up with a built-in cassette player in the teacher's desk. Each room has its own built-in overhead projector, is air-conditioned, sound-proofed, carpeted and has electric, outside-shutter blinds.

I am seeing another school next week, but most schools had their teachers sorted out by the end of the last term before they all bunked off on holiday.

AUGUST 21st:

The flat we are living in is on the second floor. Well really the second-and-a-half floor, as the ground floor is up one flight of stairs. It is a purpose-built block, constructed in the 1920s with a grey stone staircase (no lift). In the cellar we have our own little wooden caged area now full of surfboards, skis and boxes of stuff that would not fit in the flat. We are on the top floor. Above us is the attic with an area for hanging clothes up to dry. It is very good for this as it is uninsulated and gets extremely hot. This will mean in the winter we can hang clothes up to freeze. We have a caged area up there too, which is full of mattresses and more boxes of stuff that would not fit in the flat.

The flat features parquet floors which tend to creak and bounce a bit. The ceilings are a little higher than in a modern flat. The windows are mightily glazed. With the windows closed we can hear very little from outside, not even the church bells which ring for long periods at all sorts of odd times. We also have outside wooden shutters on all windows. I do not know why shutters never caught on in England. It has long been a mystery to me why, just twenty miles south of Dover, which has no working shutters, lies the start of the shutter countries. Surely the climate is no hotter or sunnier in Calais?

I describe the British as having no working shutters, as there are consid-erable quantities of non-working, or mock shutters. These have often proved to be a source of amazement and amusement to visiting Swiss, and no doubt others from the shutter-belt. These visitors to Britain often spot the problem them-selves and it normally starts with an innocent question as to why the shutters on an English house they have observed are on back to front. The louvres on shutters are designed to prevent the sun passing through them when closed. So naturally when the shutters are open and fixed to the house wall the inside of the shutter is facing outwards. To the British who dabble in mock shutters this is obviously not aesthetically pleasing. Thus they screw them to their walls – immobile and back to front.

Shutters are so practical when it is hot. No sun gets in to fade furniture and the flat is wonderfully cool and fresh when it is hot outside. When the shutters are closed we can have the windows open and safely leave them open while we are out. Rain cannot get in. And should any athletic burglar make it up the outside of the building to the second floor, the shutters would foil him. Of course shutters only work with inward opening windows and these have the bonus that you can clean the outside of the windows as easily as the inside. Shutters are also very useful if you have no, or very thin, curtains. And in the winter they add to the insulation when it is very cold.

The kitchen is quite modern with built-in oven and fridge (both Swiss made of course). Central heating is on a communal basis for the whole building of five flats and is oil-fired. Hot water is by immersion heater in the kitchen, which we put on at night when electricity is cheaper (but sometimes forget, then it's my fault). The hot and cold water are high pressure direct from the mains. So, unlike in a flat I once had in Bournemouth with miserable water pressure, we do not need to kneel down in the bath to get any water to come out of the shower. In the cellar there is a communal washing machine. Its use is on a rota system for two days every fortnight. This limitation does not worry us, but could be a problem if we had nappies for example. Happily we are both past that stage. This is a typical Swiss arrangement (the wash room, not the nappies).

AUGUST 23rd:

I bought a new pair of skis in a sale and I wanted new bindings fitted the way they are on my old skis: with a wedge of plastic under each binding to stop my feet, which tip to the outside of the foot, from making me trip. However at the shop they said they could not fit these wedges as it was illegal in Switzerland. They said if I went to Germany to have them fitted that would be OK. I got round this by bringing them my old bindings with wedges which apparently they can fit as they are not new. They sold a pair of skis, but lost the sale of some new bindings. This did not concern the sales assistant, he was more worried about following Swiss rules. Was this a brush with the Swiss mentality I have heard so much about?

Instant coffee is not popular in Switzerland and its drinking is frowned upon. It is probably considered too quick and easy to make. Instant coffee is also expensive, nearly double the UK price. But, like the window-shutter mystery, there is also the great British coffee problem: ground coffee is never as good in Britain as it is on the Continent. We have devoted considerable time and energy to this issue. In the past we have taken coffee back to England that tasted great in Switzerland. We even took Zurich tap water with us in bottles to make the coffee with. But it was never as nice in England as it was in Switzerland.

Whereas there is a great tea culture in Britain, Switzerland has none. The British can hardly believe this, but if you order tea in a café in Switzerland, you can forget a well-brewed teapot, milk jug, sugar lumps, delicate china cups and silver spoons. Instead you will be served a glass of warm water with a tea bag on a string floating in it. Fortunately, the Swiss have a considerable coffee culture. Coffee is freshly brewed from ground beans and is generally excellent, full of taste and without bitterness.

There is no need for me to want for any of those little British luxuries in Switzerland. The British daily papers arrive in Zurich at about 9.30 am. At Sfr 3.50 a copy for a sensible one and Sfr 2.50 for a silly one, my reading is often limited to what I can see on the front page at the news stands without actually buying one.

We found our favourite Tortilla Chips which cost 48p in England. In Zurich they are two and a half times as much. You can buy everything here that you can buy in England – but at a price. Even English bread – white, sliced and tasteless at £1.00 a loaf. My favourite breakfast treat, SHREDDIES, can be bought here. But the price soon weaned me off them. Retailers' margins are relatively high, and compared to the UK, there are still many small specialised shops, where the Swiss are willing to pay more for service and not buy at the cheapest price. With wages at Sfr 18 per hour to fill supermarket shelves and shopping hours from 8 am to 6.30 pm, prices have to be high. Pasta, rice and cigarettes are cheaper, so is petrol, and new cars are about 15% cheaper than the same models in Britain.

AUGUST 25th:

As the month wears on, some of the language school principals are wandering back to their desks, suitably suntanned and refreshed. One or two spotted my letter in the pile of post that awaited them, and one has even written asking to see me. The school turned out to be a rather unusual outfit by the name of Look & Learn. Why unusual? Well, they already have an English teacher, but students complain about him. He yawns and looks at his watch during the lessons. The 'lessons' are private tutorials to supplement the school's system of cassette courses. There is no language laboratory, instead the students take the tapes home to use together with books. The parent company in Germany went bust. As a result the Zurich branch is a little short of customers. However this, and the fact that there is already a teacher, means that I can start my new career as an English teacher slowly. They have offered me one hour's teaching next week, which is a little more slowly than I had envisaged.

AUGUST 30th:

I was invited by postcard to visit our local community office and told to bring two passport-sized photographs and Sfr 54. This I did. They issued the long-awaited papers. Not a work permit as such, but an identity card for foreigners granting me a residents' permit B. Permit A is for the euphemistically titled 'guest workers', who come for a season to do jobs that the Swiss will not touch, and then go back after their season is finished. Permit C is for people who have grounds for staying in Switzerland permanently, like being married to one of its citizens, and are well behaved and able to prove it by living with, and paying for, a permit B for five years.

So my permit B is the start of my probation. It already states the name of my new employers, who have to pay Sfr 40 each year to the community office for the pleasure of employing me. One cannot get a permit without a job and, as I found out, one has the greatest of difficulty in getting a job without a permit. But I have broken the 'Catch 22'. I am now a fully paid up, but as yet only associate member of one of the most exclusive clubs in the world – Switzerland.

SEPTEMBER 10th:

According to the wealth of useless information printed in my pocket diary, Switzerland and England have the same number of public holidays. This is wrong. Switzerland has more, but many of these are odd local holidays that apply to only one canton or town.

Yesterday Zurich had one. To complicate matters further it is only for an afternoon, a Monday afternoon at that. The hard working citizens of Zurich go to work on Monday morning as usual, but have the afternoon off. Can you imagine a British bank holiday on a Monday afternoon where everyone works in the morning? That is not all; wait until you hear what this holiday is for. It is called *Knabenschiessen*, which means 'boys shooting'. No they do not actually shoot the boys, they have a shooting competition for boys. Yes with real guns at targets, and Switzerland's largest city takes the afternoon off for it.

The shooting competition is accompanied by a fun fair, which is quite large considering that it is a moving one. Once you have seen one fair, you have seen them all – dodgers, waltzers, twizzers and lots of rides to make you sick and plenty of sweet food sold to do it with. We went along as it was my first time. As expected, it was expensive. I recalled the days of my youth at a seaside town. Then for 2/6 (two shillings and six pence, an amount so old and small that there is no Swiss equivalent) I could spend the whole day in the Fun House. To spend £1.50 on a three-minute ride on some Disco-Fever-Whirly-Wheeler seemed scandalous.

We have found another way to spend money. England and Switzerland have an agreement on driving licences. In England, Regula swopped her Swiss one for an English one. She filled in a form from the post office in England and sent it and her Swiss licence to Swansea. Two weeks later she had an English licence free-of-charge. The Swiss one was never to be seen again. But in Switzerland? You guessed it – getting a driving licence costs money, and of course involves plenty of paperwork.

To convert our British licences (which are valid here for only one year) into Swiss ones we have to get a certificate from an optician to say we can see, a requirement that seems ludicrous to a Brit. We must submit this, together with our papers to say we are allowed to live here, as well as passport-size photos in duplicate, then pay Sfr 70 each. I feel like not doing it. I have never had to show my licence to anyone before. My British licence is valid here for another ten months. After that I will have to take the Swiss driving test. This is in German and includes a two-hour written paper. Suddenly Sfr 70 to convert my British licence sounds like good value.

SEPTEMBER 12th:

After two weeks and three lessons at Look & Learn I have proved that I am not a complete idiot. I have not scared away the few customers they have, so they will slowly give me more students, with the emphasis on slowly. I always maintain that 50% of any job in any business or industry, is simply to turn up on time and be nice. It is surprising how many people cannot even do this. On this principle I had half of the job in the bag already. Next week I have six hours of teaching. At last I've cracked it! I am working and it is great to be paid just to talk to people in English.

SEPTEMBER 15th:

As the hours at Look & Learn have started to pick up, I have turned down the Migros job. It was poorly paid and only for one evening a week. But no sooner have I closed one door, than another one opens. Very shortly after we arrived in Switzerland my brother-in-law Andreas, who is a doctor, said that he had heard about an English teaching job through one of his patients. I had sent off one of my suitably worded letters to St. Addanuf Language School, but had heard nothing further. I assumed this was due to the Swiss holiday syndrome. That was only partly the reason for my letter going unanswered. The main reason was that the lady who runs the school single-handedly does not speak a word of English. She had my letter but could not read it, let alone answer it.

Andreas phoned me to say that he was surprised that I had not followed up his lead. I said I had, but had heard nothing, so I phoned up and made an appointment. All negotiations were conducted in German. Another touch of the *ja ja* and *natürlich*. The interview lasted about an hour. I did not say too much, because I couldn't. I asked a couple of questions. Not that I was really interested in the answers, but I knew from interviewing people myself that it is always better to seem keen and ask questions. The problem was that my German was so limited that I asked pathetic things like "How many rooms are there in the school?" and "Do the students all come to their classes on time?" I signed what I took to be an application form and we shook hands and parted amicably. I have no idea if I have got the job or not.

SEPTEMBER 18th:

I have not heard from St Addanuf Language School, but today their new brochure came out and I discovered my name in there for next term. The term starts in October and runs to April. I shall be teaching there two evenings and one afternoon per week.

A private student comes to our flat one hour a week for beginners' English. This is as a result of the card I put on the customers' free-of-charge notice board in the local supermarket. I could do with a few more of these (students, not cards). My work at Look & Learn continues to grow. They sacked their other English teacher and now I have about ten hours a week there.

SEPTEMBER 23rd

Having got our jobs sorted out and some sort of semblance of order in our flat, we look towards the mountains. For me this is one of the big attractions of living in Switzerland. I love walking and am simply potty about skiing. Autumn is the best time for walking. Temperatures are cooler, it is dry under foot and most important, the air is clear, which permits some amazing views you do not get in the heat and haze of summer. We are somewhat limited as we must travel by train, but this is only a slight limitation. Swiss trains go almost everywhere. They are clean, punctual and, unlike a certain other country I could mention, the trains run a full service not only on Sundays, but over Christmas and New Year too.

We became so used to having a car in England, not having one now is almost as if something is missing. It is so handy to look out at the weather and if it is good, simply throw our walking shoes, or skis, or windsurf board in, or on, the car and go within minutes. So, we have decided to buy a used car.

We did not have too much idea what kind of car we wanted. Regula wanted an automatic with a catalytic converter (to make it smell nice for other motorists). I wanted something reliable and big enough to take windsurf boards on and skis in. We spent a very tedious Saturday looking round car showrooms and big used-car lots. Everything we fancied was too expensive or, if affordable, very boring. In the end we found a compromise that satisfied neither of us.

We are getting a nine-year-old Opel Ascona 2.E automatic four-door saloon. The mileage is low (well kilometreage actually) at just over 2000 km – but that is because it is on its second 100,000 km, hopefully not the third. It can be left out in the street without any worries about bumps and scratched paintwork. We found our dull rust-coloured Ascona down the little road where Regula's parents live.

We had gone to their house to use their toilet on our showroom travels and her father said, "Why don't you try the man who has a little car repair business in the basement of the flats at the end of the road?"

"What" we said, "the man that gave you only 600 francs for your old Fiesta that must have been worth at least 3000??!!"

Her father clarified that the Sfr 600 offer did not come from this man. This man offered him nothing, but was good enough to offer to take the car off his hands without charging. The motor trade is the same the world over, so it seems. But Regula's mother pointed out that if this chap could buy so cheaply he may well sell some bargains – punters are the same the world over too.

The car comes complete with a set of brand new winter tyres already on a set of wheels, something essential here to get to the ski resorts in winter. The only problem will be finding somewhere to keep these wheels, as our cellar is already full to danger level with all the stuff we could not fit in our flat.

SEPTEMBER 26th:

There is no National Health system in Switzerland. But surprisingly, my health insurance is not as expensive as I had expected. It even looks like a good deal compared to paying 10% of one's salary for 'National Insurance Contributions' in the UK.

The Swiss health insurance is not earnings-related and has to be paid whether you work or not. Swiss salaries are paid gross of tax. The total deduction is around 6%, made up of state pension and unemployment benefit contribution. Unlike in the UK, where income tax is deducted as you earn, in Switzerland we are sent a bill for our taxes. This is plural, because there are a number of taxes. Sounds ominous.

OCTOBER 1st:

We have a big improvement in our getting-up-time as Regula has renegotiated her starting time from 7.30 to a very leisurely, and rather late (for Zurich), 8.30 am. She can now get a seat on the tram because fewer people start so late. This fits in better with my teaching schedule and getting up at 6.45 rather than 5.45, seems like pure luxury. Only postmen and insomniacs get up before 7 am in Britain.

I have received my first Swiss salary and have some money on my Swiss bank account for the first time. It is like starting all over again.

Some twenty years ago when I finished my first week in my very first job as a media assistant in a large London advertising agency, I was given the princely sum of £10 net. My mother enquired whether I was going to take her out for a meal with the money. £10 was a lot of money then; it is less than half an hour's worth of English teaching at today's rates. Being mean, my answer was "no".

But guess what? Regula asked me to take her out for a meal with my first Swiss salary. Again I answered "no". Maybe the third time around...

OCTOBER 3rd:

I am now the proud owner of car number plate ZH 575586. Probably the highest number in the whole Canton of Zurich for a week or two. In Switzerland the number goes with the driver, often for life. Instead of indicating how old the car is, as with the British system, it gives an idea of how old the driver is and how long he or she has been driving. Generally the lower and catchy numbers are more desirable.

British plates, which are a mixture of letters and figures, allow plenty of creative scope for spelling out names or initials. By comparison, the Swiss numbers are fairly boring.

Unlike in the UK, there is no trade in Swiss number plates and each number is prefixed with two letters to indicate the canton.

The Swiss number-plate system gives an idea how old the driver is.

I have driven in a number of countries, including Kenya, Turkey, coast to coast USA and even Paris in the rush hour. But Zurich has to be one of the most difficult places to drive in the world. My previous driving experience here was with British registered cars. The Swiss motorist, with perhaps an eye to tourist revenues, or the thought that he might one day have to drive in London, was always very tolerant and forgiving. But the moment I put Swiss plates on the car that all ended.

There is a cunning strategy against the car in Zurich. Traffic lights stay red for two minutes, then flash directly to green and allow only five cars through before turning red again for another two minutes. Motorists are encouraged to switch off their motor to cut down fumes as they wait, but woe betide anyone who is not off the mark at the flash of green. I often wondered why there were so few traffic queues in Zurich compared to London. The reason is simple: not enough cars can get into Zurich to make a decent queue.

I must remember that the blowing of a car horn is not such a big deal here as in England. Zurich is about half way between London and Rome, both in distance and in the significance of horn blowing. In Rome car horns are used much as a London driver uses say, the wipers or radio: it is just another button to press to pass the time as you sit in a holdup. But to the Englishman the car horn is akin to a gauntlet slapped in his face and then tossed at his feet. However wrong the other driver is, if you blow your horn, it will be regarded as a personal insult and appropriate action will be taken, such as continuing and exaggerating the first error. It is as though you have questioned an Englishman's parentage or the fidelity of his wife by blowing your horn at him. All you really wanted him to do was let you pass as he did 45mph on the motorway. But does he pull over? Not likely! He slows down further and stays out there for the next five miles blowing his horn back and making all the most disgusting signs and gesticulations he can devise. The Swiss sound their horns much more than the British and they do not seem to get too bothered about it. They quickly amend their ways to avoid being told off again. All I have to do is remember this when I hear a horn.

OCTOBER 6th:

We collected the car just in time to meet Mark and his wife Maggie at the airport. They have come over from England to see us and have a few days' holiday. Apparently Mark has only just finished convalescing from helping us to move and this time hopes to have a holiday here. He phoned to say that they would be on the 8.50 pm plane. We did not know this was his own calculation based on the departure time. He had not accounted for the fact that Britain is an hour behind the rest of Europe, except for a week or two each spring and autumn when British time goes on or off summer time on the same dates as the United States of all places, rather than the Continent. Come on Britain! Are you European or American?

I could have started a campaign about the use of 'Europe' in Britain many times. Politicians, so-called captains of industry and TV and radio interviewers are always referring to how we do things in Britain as opposed to how they do things "in Europe". Where do they think Britain is? In its own little self-contained continent? When I lived in England and friends said they were going to Europe for their holidays, I would ingratiate myself with them by enquiring whether this was Wales, Scotland or Ireland. This terrible insular trait of the British has been noted from time to time by more than one of my students. I dare not tell them about the famous British newspaper headline from the 1930s: "Fog in Channel – Europe cut off!"

Regula phoned the airport at 8.10 pm to see if the flight due at 20.50 was on time. She was informed that there was no flight which arrives at 20.50, but the one due at 19.50 had arrived on time. Luckily we are only about twelve minutes' drive from the airport, so Mark and Maggie only had a few minutes wandering around the terminal building thinking that we had deserted them. Maggie is what the Swiss would call a *spezielle* person. It does not have quite the same connotation as 'special' and tends more towards the odd end of unique. She has the marvellous ability to cut through the formal nonsense and niceties of normal social etiquette with a simple straight-to-the-point question. Such as "Are all the Swiss like Regula – so particular and fussy?" I said they were usually much worse and that is how they get the trains to run on time and can serve first-class meals at any time of day on the top of most mountains.

Seeing the order and tidiness of Switzerland, Maggie asked Regula "Are there any prisons in Switzerland?" I think she felt that Switzerland was a bit of a police state with little freedom and no crime, which is true to a certain extent. Her impression was greatly enhanced as we drove back from the airport. I left the autobahn on an exit road that runs into a residential street with a 50kph speed limit. Suddenly the car was lit up with two bright flashes. I had gone past a 'metal policeman', an automatic radar trap which photographed the car and my shiny new rear number plate. These radar traps are big sturdy grey metal boxes which are sprinkled liberally over the Swiss road system. They do not always contain a camera, but there is only one way to find out... This is why most Swiss drivers keep rigorously to the speed limits. They also rarely go below them either, which makes motorway driving more restful than in England where you need to keep passing vehicles going at 50mph. Most drive here at about 125kph on the autobahn, which is just 5kph over the limit and about 80mph. The speed limit was lowered from 130kph some years ago.

Maggie was impressed and wondered if the police with cameras were everywhere in Switzerland waiting to photograph felons. I replied "Not yet". After being photographed by the radar trap, we photographed some tourist traps with Mark and Maggie and, four days later, delivered them carefully back to the airport at central European time and within the speed limit.

OCTOBER 11th:

I was disappointed with the speed of Swiss cash dispensers. In England I could get my cash out in eighteen seconds. (I know, I timed it.) Here the dispenser is rather slow and ponderous. But, having asked for all communication to be in English when I opened the account, I find now that this also applies to the cash dispenser which has a little TV screen on it. It chats to Regula in German and to me in English. Even the printed receipt it gives out is in the language which the customer requested. Maybe it needs time for translation?

October is generally an excellent month in Switzerland weather-wise. It turns cooler, and very clear. It is still warm enough to sit outside in the sun. Misty mornings give way to glorious sunny afternoons with golden leaves. From Zurich we can see the snow-capped mountains now. This is the first time we have seen them from here since we arrived. They were hiding all summer in heat haze. The views while walking in the mountains are stupendous. This is the time to walk. The only problem is that half the population thinks so too.

This clear weather is often caused by a great Alpine invention, the *Föhn* (pronounced somewhere between 'fern' and 'phone'). This is a wind which comes over the Alps from the Mediterranean. *Föhn* is also the German for hair drier, so you get some idea of what it is like. Usually, when a low pressure storm system is on its way from the British Isles, air pressure drops and air is sucked over the mountain passes from the south. Rather like a big wave approaching a beach first sucks pebbles out to sea.

As the air is forced up the south faces of the mountains, it loses its moisture. When it drops down the north side of the Alps, it expands and warms up, sometimes dramatically. It can be very localised and occur only in a few valleys. One valley might have rain and be only 10°C, while in the next valley the *Föhn* brings a perfect sunny day and 20°. Or the *Föhn* can blow over the whole of northern Switzerland and beyond. It can be a very short-lived wind and switch on and off just like a hair drier. The *Föhn* is also associated with headaches, and the suicide and accident rates actually go up when it is blowing. The British always blame the government for all their ills, but the Swiss blame the *Föhn*.

OCTOBER 16th:

I have now started at the second school, St. Addanuf. Teaching certainly is a challenge with beginners, which all my five classes are. Of the sixty or so students there is only one who cannot speak a single word of English. He told me so in German. But I intend to change that. He is going to speak at least one by Christmas, or my name is not Santa Claus.

OCTOBER 17th:

I have driven for twenty-four years without ever getting a speeding ticket. But now, before I had driven twenty kilometres in our new car, I was photographed doing a glorious 66kph in a 50kph zone. The fine has arrived. They did not even send the picture. Five kph was deducted for speedometer error. The police say I was 11kph over the limit and have fined me Sfr 100. From now on I stick to speed limits (or keep my number plate dirty). I confess that I have previously been photographed here a number of times while speeding in British cars, but I got away with it. Fines for minor speeding infractions are not always sent to offenders who live outside of Switzerland.

OCTOBER 25th:

I ordered a thousand little stickers printed with our new Swiss address, but I am now reluctant to use them on the back of letters as they tell the postman too much. I bought the wrong stamps by mistake for letters to Blighty. So I thought 'what the 'eck' and sent a letter with stamps ten *Rappen* too little. (*Rappen* or cent. 100 *Rappen* = Sfr 1.)

Today there was a printed postcard in our letter box (we have a box in the wall by the front door) from the PTT (post office). It said that I had not put enough stamps on the letter. Nevertheless they had sent it on as a gesture of goodwill, but would I please attach a 10 *Rappen* stamp to the post card and put it back in the mail. "Gulp," I thought "they've got me here. Maggie was right – somebody will be round to beat me up if I don't comply." But it was only part of the meticulous Swiss attention to detail. It is the way they keep the trains, and everything else, running on time. Mind you, when the road is clear, I still cross the road when the man is red. But I have heard that accident insurance pay-outs can be cut by up to 40% if an accident with a car occurs because the pedestrian crossed on red.

OCTOBER 29th:

We went on an organised tour of the old town of Zurich, given in English by a Czechoslovakian. (I think this is taking 'guest working' too far.) The tour was simple, but nevertheless showed us parts of the town we had not seen before and we learned some facts about Zurich we did not know. Over the centuries Zurich seems to have been a town much as today; that is rather clean, tidy, efficient and somewhat boring. Wars and revolutions were rare and everyone worked and saved hard and did rather well thank you very much. The last great exciting thing that happened was when the Romans came here to open a bank account and named the town Turicum. They probably could not pronounce Zurich. Today the old town is so 'licked' (that is, too clean and tidy) that none of the old buildings are in their original state. They may look like it from the outside, except for the double-glazed windows, but inside there are expensive modern flats, houses, shops and restaurants with air conditioning, cable TV, and wall-to-wall tidiness.

NOVEMBER 6th:

I have never been a big fan of autumn, but Switzerland did its best to change that for me with such a glorious October. November, however, is another matter. November is definitely the month to go on holiday to the

Caribbean. I can always recall not having a particular liking for November. Guy Fawkes was probably of the same opinion. Thanks to him, in my earlier years, the month was at least partly salvaged by containing Bonfire Night. That novelty soon paled when I had to fork out for my fireworks myself. The Swiss let their fireworks off on August 1st, leaving November a sparkle-less month.

The *Föhn* is now just a fond memory. It is cold (about 6°C maximum), overcast and drizzling. It is too cold to even think of windsurfing and still a good month away from any skiing. Regula is pragmatic about it and says it is an ideal month for shopping, particularly with Christmas around the corner. But I always like to leave Christmas shopping until it is far too late. I am glad to see that there is, as yet, no sign of Christmas in the Zurich shops, we saw on the TV that the Christmas lights have already been switched on in London's Oxford Street. It was the joke item at the end of the Swiss news.

The seasons are better defined here than in southern England, where one has to check the calendar to see what season it is, as it is impossible to tell by the weather. Some friends from Australia visited with their children one August in England. As we were driving through the countryside in somewhat murky, dull British-August weather, a small voice with thick Australian accent was heard to enquire quite seriously, "Dad, is this summer or winter here?" In Switzerland we are left in little doubt, as the seasons are very different. The summers warmer and the winters colder. I have had to buy a new long winter coat (for long winters) as it is so cold.

NOVEMBER 10th:

The autumn leaves are nearly all off the trees, but do the Swiss have lots of smoky bonfires to get rid of their leaves? This is the great curse of November in rural England. Do Swiss fires pollute the air and annoy neighbours? Need I ask? Swiss gardeners fill plastic sacks with them (the leaves that is, not the neighbours) and then once a week a lorry comes round and takes them away to the community's great compost heap.

Switzerland has a number of unique institutions that seem to work perfectly well here, but would be a recipe for disaster elsewhere. Switzerland is so neutral that it does not even have a seat in the United Nations. Many people misunderstand Switzerland's neutrality. It is not an undefended land of pacifists. On the contrary, it is 'aggressively' neutral with a large and successful arms industry. Switzerland is heavily defended with its army of 600,000 soldiers. All of them are armed with much more than just Swiss Army Knives.

Neither would you expect this to be any old army. The Swiss require that every able-bodied male citizen from twenty to about forty be involved in the army. This can be extended to sixty in the army reserves. All these men have their uniforms in their wardrobes at home and their guns and ammunition in a kitchen or attic cupboard. Can you imagine Saturday nights in any British town with this potential arsenal in everybody's home?

When riding on the tram or train in Switzerland one often sees men, sometimes not even in uniform, carrying rifles or submachine guns. They are just off for a bit of shooting practice. After an initial training, they serve a period of three weeks each year, reducing to two weeks later. From what I can gather, these periods of military service are quite good fun, particularly if the weather is nice. They have also led to a sort of 'old school tie network' of promotion and 'jobs for the boys' in civilian industry and commerce.

NOVEMBER 13th:

As the name 'Confoederatio Helvetica' suggests, Switzerland is a confederation rather than a single country as the British understand it. It is a confederation of fiercely independent cantons, each with its own folklore and traditions.

These cantons not only speak different dialects (not to mention languages) and eat their own food specialities, they appoint their own public holidays, raise their own taxes and run their own education systems. In turn the cantons are, in theory at least, run by the inhabitants. This is done through a voting system which could be interpreted as either heaven on earth, or democracy gone mad. I say 'in theory' as I remember seeing some graffiti sprayed on a wall in Zurich which summed up the situation quite well (in perfect English): "If voting made any difference they wouldn't let us vote."

Every Swiss national over the age of eighteen is entitled to vote on whatever there is to vote about at the time. And yes, women are allowed to vote (as they have been since 1971), but foreigners cannot. In English most of these votes would really be called referendums or plebiscites. There was only one in Britain in my lifetime and that was to join the Common Market.

The Swiss vote about something every three months. The subjects range from national items, cantonal, town or even local community issues. Thus before any major expenditure is made for roads, building bridges, schools and hospitals, it has to be approved first by the people. In addition, if a group of citizens can collect enough signatures, they can get their own vote going. For example, a committee of like-minded persons determined to disband the hallowed institution of the Swiss army gets a vote going on this issue every few years. Each time the result is closer and there is another vote on it on December 5th. These campaigns often involve a great deal of publicity and advertising in the weeks running up to the vote. Hours on TV and radio are devoted to discussing the pros and cons. And the ballot papers are not the easiest things to understand. They are supplied in advance. Voters study the issues carefully, read the official recommendations, and learn how the politicians have already voted on the various subjects. It's all taken very seriously.

Also up for the people's decision is a proposal to raise the autobahn speed limit back up to 130kph. It was reduced to 120kph without a vote some years ago to reduce air pollution. Perhaps the graffiti writer was right, for it seems for all the outward show of democracy, when the government or the authorities want something, they do it without a vote. Even when the people have voted 'yes' to a proposal that is against the authorities' political views, somehow the money cannot be found to do it, or it is delayed in the hope of another vote reversing the decision.

NOVEMBER 15th:

The value of the pound continues to slide downwards (pound sterling, £, British pound or 'quid', but please never English pound, although there is a Scottish pound – got it?) It has already fallen over 5% in the few months that we have been here. When Regula was an au-pair in England in the late sixties, there were Sfr 8 to the pound and when her father first went to London in the early 1950s there were an amazing Sfr 14 to the pound. That is why inflation has been nearly nonexistent in Switzerland. Or is it because of low inflation that the currency has risen? Either way the rise in the exchange rate against the pound has made Switzerland so expensive for the British, but the same as always for the Swiss.

NOVEMBER 29th:

The mobile telephone craze (or is it curse) has hit Switzerland hard. The Swiss are very good at taking up new ideas, while at the same time holding on to some good old-fashioned traditions. But this telephone business is getting out of control. People can be seen everywhere talking into their hands. As I travel on the tram I often look down into cars stuck at red lights, their drivers phoning ahead to say they will be late. In the tram itself, passengers answer phones that ring in their pockets. Even the driver of the dustcart has one in his cab. I suppose if he misses a plastic bag they can phone him up to go back for it. I have a student who wears a dinky little one on his belt and rushes out into the corridor to answer it when it rings. A man Regula works for has a phone in his car, but he only ever calls her to see if it is still working. How did these people ever survive B.C. (Before Cellnet)? The Swiss version is not called Cellnet, but Natel after its inventor, William Na-Tell!

DECEMBER 4th:

November was best swept quickly aside. Sadly this was of little advantage though, as December picked up the gauntlet and started in an all too familiar dull, cold and grey fashion with zero degree temperatures and fog every day. But today it changed completely and now our old friend the *Föhn* came back – giving temperatures up to 20°C! Although snow is forever being forecast there has been virtually no snow in the mountains at all.

Why is this man worrying about the lack of snow? If this is what you are thinking, then I must sadly conclude that you are not a skier. Previously I waxed lyrical about windsurfing; well I suppose I should do the same about skiing. However, I feel that enough people ski already and if I encouraged any more it would simply impair the enjoyment of existing skiers. Sorry.

DECEMBER 5th:

The Swiss voted: the army will not be disbanded and the speed limit will remain at 120kph. The Swiss are so sensible. Can you imagine this system working in Britain? A few years ago the Swiss even voted against a proposal to reduce the standard working week from forty-two hours. I am sure the British with the same system would vote themselves endless holidays and free beer on the National Health.

DECEMBER 6th:

Today is *Samichlaustag* – St. Nicholas's day. All wacky people dressed as St. Nicholas (i.e. Father Christmas) can travel free on Zurich's transport system. I did not see any takers. However I did see a bright red little tram with lights all over it driven by St. Nicholas himself. Parents take their children to see St. Nicholas in such diverse places as department stores and his house in the woods as well as on his tram. There is a big demand for St. Nicholases to come round to people's homes and amuse or scare the children as the case may be. A family friend can do this or one can always be rented from the official St. Nicholas Trade Union.

Oh yes, training and apprenticeships in Switzerland apply to every walk of life and even St. Nicholas has to be trained. He has to know how to handle children and what is emotionally harmful to them. There is more to it than just putting on a red suit and white beard and ho-ho-ho-ing. He is traditionally accompanied by a donkey and a rather dirty assistant. St. Nicholas deals out sweets and nuts to good children and whacks bad ones with a bundle of twigs. This is, of course, psychologically damaging to children and so these days he sticks to being nice and giving away things.

This may sound rather disappointing to children used to piles of presents on Christmas morning, but, never fear, the *Christkind* does this and kids do not even have to wait until Christmas Day because the Christ Child turns up with the goodies on Christmas Eve.

When Regula arrived at work this morning, the offices were full of things left by *Samichlaus*, including lots of *Grittibänz* (bread in the shape of a man), as well as nuts, oranges and even balloons and ribbons. Apparently one of the office cleaners does this each year – the things some people do to get a tip at Christmas.

DECEMBER 10th:

The dreaded Swiss tax form arrived with a bump. We first got a registered letter from the tax people saying that if we did not return the form they sent us a month ago they would come round and break our legs (I am sure it was something like that, my German is still very shaky). So Regula called them and said we had not received a form and one was then duly dispatched.

In Britain the level of income tax is national and exactly the same wherever you live in the UK, with the exception of the Channel Isles and the Isle of Man. The Swiss tax system is local. People in the town of Zurich pay all their taxes to the Zurich office and only a percentage is forwarded for central government. The level of taxation varies from community to community within each canton. Thus each town and village has a different level of taxation and one is taxed where one lives, not where one works.

The Swiss tax system is not a 'pay as you earn' one as in the UK. Salaries are paid gross and one must account for, and then pay, the taxes by the end of the year. In practice this means that you pay an estimate in the first year and then taxes in the next based on the previous year's declaration. The Swiss tax office allows you to pay your tax bill in three or four instalments through the year, so that it is not too scary in the 'large-bills-at-Christmas' department.

Naturally, being Switzerland, the tax form asks for all sorts of seemingly irrelevant information not required by the British authorities, like our birth dates (perhaps they will send us cards?) It is a Swiss preoccupation to require one's date of birth on all forms. If you check into a Swiss hotel, after your name on the registration card, they ask for your date of birth.

I bought a pair of Swiss ski-trousers which have a sewn-in label to write in my name, date of birth and address. If my body is found in a glacial crevasse, they will have a head start with my obituary. I've lied about my age, though.

We were getting quite bogged down with the tax form and the accompanying twenty-page explanation. It looked as though the ten days' deadline would not be enough – but then Regula's father came to the rescue. He sharpened his pencil and steamed through the form like a seasoned Swiss form-filler. The taxation principles are not dissimilar to those in the UK about forty years ago. All sorts of unexpected things can be set against tax – clothes and books for one's work – there is even an allowance of Sfr 4 for lunch and Sfr 8 for dinner per day for people who work. No wonder we can never get a seat in a restaurant. Our season tickets for the tram, already a bargain, are tax deductible. Mortgages are allowable, as many as you want and without limit. I must make sure we have a few next time.

I wrote to the British Inland Revenue before we left England advising that we were going abroad. Now, six months later they have sent a letter which, despite being in English, I cannot understand. They have had to refer my case to Head Office, which they always seem to do. In their wisdom they wrote to advise that for the time being I will continue to be regarded as 'Resident and Ordinarily Resident' in the UK. This is apparently because it depends not only on my intentions but whether these intentions are carried out. The situation will be reviewed again in eighteen months.

At least they do not seem to want a year's tax from me as I feared. I would have thought that it is impossible to carry out the intention of living abroad more clearly than we have. They seem to want to see what I am up to before committing themselves on paper.

DECEMBER 21st:

A very strange Zurich tradition came to light in the early hours of this morning. I was woken by Regula turning the light on and saying "No, it's far too early!"

I had to agree, it was 3 am. Then I heard what sounded like gunfire. Had invading hoards landed and was this the sound of hand to hand fighting in the streets? Had the Swiss army actually been called upon to use the guns they keep at home?

Regula was now sitting up in bed and listening. "No, no they aren't supposed to start until 5 am." She seemed to be on the winning side and knew all their plans. That was some relief I suppose. But what was it? Well it was nothing more or less than the old local tradition of 'School Silvester'. Every one of the 365 days of the year is also called after a Christian and the last day of the year, December 31st, is the name day of Silvester. So New Year's Eve is known in Switzerland as 'Silvester'. Thus, the last day of the year at school is known as School Silvester.

It has been a tradition for many years in the town of Zurich. On the last day of school before Christmas the school kids get up very early in the morning and roam the streets letting off fireworks, ringing cow bells, hitting pan lids together, shouting and generally making as much noise as possible. It is a fairly official thing as it is mentioned in the paper the day before, which Regula promptly got out and looked up the details. "Yes of course it says here: 'No fireworks'." So school kids, who had never thought of letting fireworks off before, were given a great idea.

What goes on at this end-of-term party? There is a disco starting at 4 am – that's right, it STARTS at four in the morning! It could only happen in Switzerland. There was also a warning in the paper not to leave your plastic rubbish sacks out in the street overnight. Presumably in the event they could find no fireworks, the children would let those off instead.

I had only heard of Silvester in relation to New Year's Eve. When I asked Regula what Silvester meant, she said of course it was the black cat that chased the little canary (thuffering thuckertash). When Regula's mother used to do this Silvester business in her school days, they would arrange to meet in the early hours and go round and collect all their class mates from their homes. The last one up was then dressed in a nightshirt and paraded through the town in a hand cart to the accompaniment of a great deal of cheering, football rattles etc. Ah, those were the days.

School holidays have come for me too. I received a number of Christmas presents from an assortment of crawlers in my classes – chocs, wine, calendars etc. The best was a bottle of 'yer actual' French Champagne – I must make sure that they get top marks next term.

Continuing the perks and bribes department, Regula got a large pack of fresh smoked salmon from the travel agent her company deals with. A few months ago she won a return flight to Paris from this company. There was a problem though. (No, it was not a one-way-ticket.) There was no accommodation and it was only for one person.

As Regula does not like travelling alone and sleeping on the streets of Paris, she gave it to Andreas for his fortieth birthday. If he is not up to sleeping on the streets of Paris now he is forty, he can pass it on to someone else. It seems like the perfect present. There is no time limit on the offer and it is an impressive gift to give anyone. No doubt it can be passed on for years and save thousands in presents. Nobody will ever actually use the ticket and so it will not even cost the travel agent anything either.

DECEMBER 24th:

Our first winter in Switzerland is going to go down as the mildest on record. The Swiss are among the world's greatest worriers and, apart from relating tales of financial disaster from empty winter resorts, the papers are full of how this is the greenhouse effect in action. All very depressing stuff for a keen skier. But I see from the weather reports we get on CNN that the United States is experiencing very cold weather and even a white Christmas is being forecast for Florida. We are not dreaming of a white Christmas anymore, we would be very happy with a white January or February.

I am developing a theory about world weather brought about by watching America's weather while sitting in the middle of a very mild Europe. Maybe the total temperature of the world is always constant. If we added together all the temperature readings from everywhere, they would always come to the same total. So when it is warmer than usual on one part of the globe, it must be cooler than normal somewhere else to compensate. Thus the sooner America's weather is back to normal, the sooner ours will be colder with snow.

DECEMBER 25th:

This is not my first Christmas in Switzerland. We have alternated our Christmases between England and Switzerland for the last seven years. I am well prepared for the low-key Swiss version of this holiday. Much closer to the original meaning of holiday – holy day. Christmas in Switzerland is very different from the UK version. For the Swiss it is generally a quiet family time. The revelry of an English Christmas with party hats and crackers is a shock for the Swiss. There is no place for these at their Christmas.

The Swiss light real candles on real trees. The mixture of fire and fir is a recipe for disaster and was abandoned years ago by the boisterous British at Christmas. However, the careful Swiss have careful Christmases and so are allowed candles and hardly ever seem to burn down their houses at Yuletide. The wild celebrations and party hats come out at New Year's Eve, which is the time when the Swiss party and when the English are never really quite sure what to do.

DECEMBER 26th:

The Swiss, as you might expect, work between Christmas and New Year whenever possible. They really only take a holiday *en masse* when the two holidays fall in such a way as to allow no alternative.

We have been very kindly invited for the New Year holiday to join some English friends at their holiday flat in the French ski resort of Val d'Isere. It could well be that we will drive up to 1800 metres (6000 ft) above sea level just to play TRIVIAL PURSUITS or SCRABBLE as the Alps are at present green and wet.

DECEMBER 30th:

Busking (the playing of music in public places for money) is getting out of hand in Zurich. Down the main shopping street it is impossible to be out of earshot of one street musician or another, from Scottish bagpipes to South American ten-piece bands. On our way back from booking some cinema tickets (yes, it is possible to buy cinema tickets in advance in Switzerland and so you should at Sfr 15 a seat) there was even a busker on the tram. An Englishman with a guitar and mouth organ (aha, that's what happened to Donovan). He got a lot of money in his hat by singing a rocking version of Silent Night.

JANUARY 1st – 5th:

The New Year found us searching in vain for decent snow at Val d'Isere in the French Alps and ruining my new skis bought as such a bargain in the summer sales.

The French treat their mountains differently from the Swiss. There is a strong environmental lobby in Switzerland and development in the Swiss Alps is now limited. But in France the bulldozer is king. This can be a shock if you are used to little chalets with overhanging roofs and cosy farming villages. Val d'Isere's ribbon development gives it a Klondike gold-rush atmosphere – a boom town, with booming discos and fast food all too common.

Why on earth did we go there, when there are perfectly good Alps in Switzerland? The answer is that we were kindly invited to stay with English friends, Grahame and Diana, who have a choice apartment in the centre of Val d'Isere. He is a property developer and he bought it obeying the three most important features you should look for in a property when buying: "position, position and position".

After buying, not property, but a couple of postcards in Val d'Isere, I thought I should try my very rusty French when I bought the stamps. Preparing myself with suitable gesticulations and pursing my lips to exaggerate my French accent, I summoned all my powers of mimicry to try and appear as Gallic as a local. At the post office counter I trotted out nonchalantly as I thought any Val d'Iseran would: *"Deux timbre-postes, s'il vous plaît"*.

The lady behind the counter opened her stamp folder and I thought all had gone well. But she paused and looked at me. *"Pour l'Angleterre, n'est-ce pas?"*

Quick as a flash I threw her off the trail by replying in English: "No, for Switzerland, actually!"

On the last day we decided to go to nearby Tigne and up the Grande Motte – 3600 metres high (nearly 11,000ft). The snow up there was deep and crisp and even. But there was a queue of about an hour at the bottom as every Tom, Dick and 'Ari wanted to go up there and make his mark on that good snow. As we arrived at the queue for the cabin, our friends met a ski instructor they knew from previous years and she very kindly took us through with her class to the front of the queue. Ski schools have a priority lane which gets them to the front of lift queues.

The ski instructor was going home the next day to Annecy (about two hours down the valley and on our way home). I offered her a lift and she very gladly accepted. We took her and her five-year-old son with his goldfish in an open bowl back down the valley (and never spilled a drop). She was a mogul expert (bump jumper) and had been European Champion in 1981. She was now a champion queue jumper.

JANUARY 6th:

It's *Dreikönigstag*, that is to say Three Kings' Day and the Swiss shops are full of 'Three Kings' Cakes'. This is a sweet bun or tea-cake containing sultanas. It is made from a number of separate pieces of dough baked together. The cake can easily be pulled apart and one of the pieces has a tiny plastic king in it, so the cake is eaten carefully.

The person who gets the king is allowed to wear a golden paper crown which comes with the cake. At the same time this lucky person is allowed to boss about the rest of the family for the day. We were shopping in a large American-style shopping mall just out of the town of Zurich, and sure enough there were children all over the place wearing these crowns round the shops. And just as the Swiss are able to light real candles on their Christmas trees and not burn their homes to the ground, so there are no tales of children choking to death on the little plastic kings found in the Three Kings' Cake.

Maybe we British have some fatal attraction to objects of potential danger. Take the British three-pin plug on electric appliances. There is nothing quite like it in the rest of the world. Massive, fused and idiot-proof. Are the British so careless with things electrical that they need this special protection? The Swiss are quite content to stick thin, flimsy round-pin plugs in their similarly flimsy sockets, even in their bathrooms. No British household can run a hair drier, or any other appliance, in their bathroom other than a shaver from a safety socket.

Lifts are the same. British TV consumer programmes are liberally scattered with grizzly tales of British kids in Spanish lifts who were somehow able to lose a limb or two because the lift had no inner door. There are lifts like this all over Switzerland in public places and shops and, guess what, nobody ends up in the casualty department instead of ladies' fashions.

Also what is it that British kids eat that makes them put plastic bags over their heads? British plastic bag manufacturers have to put holes in their bags so these hapless children can breathe during a bag-on-the-head attack. Warnings are printed on the bags so that parents do not hand plastic bags to their children to play with during a lapse in concentration.

The Swiss, on the other hand, seem blissfully unaware of these dangers of modern life that lurk in lifts and in an object as seemingly innocent as a plastic bag. Still, they probably have many other things to worry about.

JANUARY 24th:

The British weather usually turns up in Switzerland a day or so later for us to use second-hand. Thanks to storms that nearly blew away the British Isles last week, it has snowed in the Alps at last. Sadly not soon enough for five friends from England who came over to the French part of Switzerland for some 'skiing'. When I met up with them, they had been walking, mountain bike riding, playing tennis and tiddlywinks in the very green mountains.

At dinner in the evening someone asked me if a place called Kloten was near where we lived. This turned out to be a loaded question. I brightly said yes – it is where Zurich's airport is, about twelve minutes by car from us. They had some presents with them for a former English language student, Hansruedi, who had lodged with them in England for six months some ten years ago. They had kept in touch and somehow thought that by coming skiing 250 kilometres away from Zurich in the French part of Switzerland, they would be able to get some belated Christmas gifts to Hansruedi and his family. They were right, because I agreed to contact him and deliver their presents. This former student was now a restaurateur of considerable repute and I was told that I would be lavishly entertained on the house.

I had not counted on a) the sense of direction of the English and b) the frugality of the Swiss. The restaurant was neither near Kloten nor was dinner free. Hansruedi had spent six months in England to learn English, but I do not know what he did there. On the phone he said my German was so good that we had the whole conversation in German. He gave me directions how to get there. 'There' being about 25km past Kloten, just near the German border.

My German is obviously not so hot as we got completely lost and I had to phone him again. It was a very typical Swiss restaurant, serving large portions of excellent food at sensible prices, which we paid. At least we got a free dessert.

The standard of food served in restaurants is high throughout Switzerland. We have eaten in luxurious hotels and huts in the mountains. We cannot say that we have never had a duff meal, but the food is remarkably good. Portions are generous, quality high and the choice extensive. Like all big cities, the service in Zurich restaurants can be offhand. Prices nevertheless are high. Gone are the days when we could pop out to our local Italian restaurant in England for a pizza and a bottle of house plonk as a cheap meal. Here the same treat costs twice as much.

If you want something more exotic like a Chinese meal, which is very up-market and not so common in Switzerland, then you had better be sure to fill your wallet before you fill your stomach. Regula, as always, is there to remind me that Swiss wages are much higher and, by that reasoning, eating out is cheaper here than in England.

JANUARY 29th:

Whoever supplies ready-mixed concrete to the Swiss building trade has had thirty or so very profitable years. I have never seen a country with so much grey concrete. From flyovers to churches, concrete has been used with such liberality that I can only conclude that someone somewhere must find it attractive.

Regula's father is a keen amateur musician and plays the violin. We went to hear him play with his local orchestra in a Catholic church on Sunday evening. The church was a better example of the use of concrete; a subtle blend of concrete and natural wood. Certainly better than one or two others we have seen which look as though they were dedicated to St. Ment the Rigid, the patron saint of concrete suppliers. The thing which spoilt this particular church was the over-the-top electronic hymn-number board with digital figures that glowed an eerie green.

FEBRUARY 1st:

Regula now realises that her job is not the ideal one for her. The hours are long and the work is repetitive and not challenging. She wants to change, but she is so busy at work that she does not have time to look for a new job. They are not daft these Swiss employers, are they?

FEBRUARY 3rd:

I've discovered another Swiss language. It's not a complete language, but soon it might be. This language uses English words but, to make it more fun, the words don't mean the same in Switzerland. Confused? I am. Take the English noun 'food'. In this new language food becomes a verb, *fooden,* meaning to eat. But some nouns remain nouns and just have their meaning changed. Thus *pins* are not what you use to hold cloth together when sewing, but metal lapel-badges, on a multitude of themes, which are a big craze in Switzerland.

Another example is the track-suit, once used only by men and women in sports, but now half of Britain does their shopping in them. In this new Swiss language, a track-suit becomes a *trainer.* Whereas in English a trainer is either a person who trains athletes, or half a pair of running shoes.

The language is Swinglish – half Swiss half English. It should not be mistaken for the real English that is thrown into most sentences Swiss people speak. Words like 'know-how', 'insider tip', 'ticket', 'meeting' and 'last but not least' rather sadly, 'fixer'. 'Sorry' is English whereas *sorry, gäll?* (sorry, isn't it?) could be classed as Swinglish.

As German does not differentiate between a town and a city, long ago the Swiss put the word 'city' to use. *City* in Swinglish means city centre, or downtown. So Zurich tends to be referred to in English as the town of Zurich, rather than the city of Zurich, even though it is more than big enough to be one.

FEBRUARY 5th:

After a long three months of cold and gloom in Zurich, we had a Sunday afternoon when the *Föhn* blew and it was mild, clear and sunny for a few hours. We seized the opportunity and went for a walk in the hills near Zurich, taking Regula's parents with us. They went for a half-hour stroll to a restaurant, while we did a three-hour walk. When we came to the restaurant we had arranged to meet at, we found it was closed.

We could see her parents in the distance walking a bit higher up the hill. Regula shouted a sort of Swiss lowlander's yodel to them, which sounds to all the world like "coo-ee". They shouted a similar response and gave us a big wave.

As we got closer I could see that Regula's father was trailing behind and limping. He had left us quite fit some three hours earlier and, for the first time in his life, he was puffing on a cigar. Regula had to confess that the reply to her 'coo-ee' was not quite the same as she remembered when a child. As they approached, we started to express grave doubts to each other about their identity.

We managed to get to our car and were about to make a smart get-away, when this pair of bemused strangers caught up with us. They explained that they had mistaken us for some other people they had seen earlier. In the meantime the real in-laws had been to a sanatorium on the same hill and managed to get a couple of cups of coffee in the canteen.

FEBRUARY 7th:

Hardly a winter goes by without some new terror-flu threat and in Switzerland it is no different. The Swiss have plans in hand for a five-level flu alert. At level five, when the flu gets really bad, the army takes over the running of electric plants, trains etc. How do they know the army will not get the flu too?

Speaking of the army, Regula's other brother, Hannes, has twice had his stint in the army cancelled due to lack of snow – he is in the much feared and respected snowball commandoes.

FEBRUARY 11th – 17th:

More storms, which seem to be Britain's biggest export to Switzerland, brought snow in time for us to enjoy the great Swiss tradition, 'sports holidays'. In St. Moritz (where else is there?), we found the best snow of the season and not a cloud in the sky for the whole week. We had a Japanese ski instructor, who could only speak a few words of English and otherwise Japanese. He had quite a

sense of humour. Once we met some Swiss people who had stopped to sunbathe on their way down the Morteratsch Glacier. They were surprised to see a Japanese ski instructor. He reacted to their surprise by asking them if he was going in the right direction for Tokyo.

He was so earnest and serious, that they felt obliged to inform him in English that he was lost. He was often prone to long periods of silence and some sort of inner meditation. When he did speak, we had great difficulty understanding him. Once, after a long silence and gaze at the mountains, he drew a deep breath and stared at us intently. Then he declared what sounded to us like "Now we go suicide!" We looked at each other and were just about to depart for an early bath when one of the group realised that we were on a slope out of the sun and what he actually meant was "now we go sunny side".

At lunch one day we made various toasts in assorted languages we knew. One woman in our group, a small and rather husky Dutch lady, said that she knew a toast in English we had all missed. We could not think of any more. She then proceeded to slowly and solemnly raise her glass. Having captured our attention, she rasped the familiar but wholly inappropriate words "up yours!" It took us about ten minutes to stop laughing before we could explain to her the error of her ways.

FEBRUARY 19th:

No sooner had we finished a perfect week's skiing than the umpteenth storm from Britain reached us with torrential rain and high winds. Switzerland is not accustomed to winds of any sort, let alone storms (as I found out trying to windsurf here). Thus when the Swiss want to refurbish a building inside and out (which seems to apply to about 25% of the buildings here at any one time), they cover the whole building with a large plastic bag over the scaffolding. This stops the neighbours from looking in and it keeps dirt, dust and flying objects from injuring passers-by.

It also enables a large hot-air heater to be stuck through the plastic so that the Turkish workers can work merrily in the coldest of Swiss winters just as though they were working in the height of a Mediterranean summer.

Why don't we do this in England? Because the plastic bags would soon be ripped to shreds in a most spectacular fashion, as happened here in the storm. The same applies to shutters, which could be seen flapping wildly and uncontrollably, and in one case actually smashing the windows they are supposed to protect.

FEBRUARY 23rd:

The next event on the Zurich calendar is *Fasnacht*, or 'fast night' (much better than a slow one), and is just before the start of Lent, hence the reference to fasting. It is a sort of carnival and it is taken very seriously.

Whereas in Rio they stay up late and dance nearly naked in hot weather, in Switzerland they get up at 5 am, or earlier, on a cold black winter morning and then wake everyone else up – sounds like great fun! *Fasnacht* officially starts on the eleventh of November, the eleventh month, at 11.11 am. But it does not really get into its stride until February. Folk from many towns spend a lot of time and effort on *Fasnacht*. This involves dressing up in exotic and eccentric costumes with masks and painted faces, producing satirical songs and playing music off-key on purpose.

For me the best part is travelling on the tram when carnival participants are on their way to meet up with the rest of their group. The tram doors open and in walks a middle-aged woman dressed as a clown complete with bright orange fuzzy wig, white face with red nose and a large painted smile. Atop her head is a pointed hat and her outfit is a perfect white and red polka-dot baggy clown's suit with frilly cuffs and neck. Do the discretely yet fashionably-dressed passengers all swing round to look at her as she takes her seat? Do fingers point and children giggle? No, nobody even bats an eyelid.

MARCH 7th:

February blew into March and my sister Angie and her family came over for a rather hectic weekend's skiing. It was their first time on skis. The weather looked very unsettled when they arrived on the Friday. But Saturday and Sunday turned out to be two glorious days with bright sunshine and the best snow this winter – nice and new and deep. They seemed to be magnetically attracted to the snow and found hundreds of ways of falling into it. We introduced them to the delights of 'apres ski' and even 'avant ski' in the form of *Kaffee fertig* (coffee and schnaps) as well as the Swiss equivalent of fish and chips; *Rösti* with two fried eggs on top. They were bitten by the skiing bug.

MARCH 11th:

I met up with some more English pals for a day in their ski holidays at Klosters, about an hour-and-a-half's drive from Zurich. We had a very nice day, but Charles was not there (our next king, a previous king of that name having been named after a Spaniel and another lost his head (but not while skiing)). His Royal Avalancheness had been seen there twice that week, but he got out of town when I came along.

MARCH 24th:

A sudden burst of warm sweet-smelling air from the Mediterranean converted winter into a mild sunny spring. And naturally at such a time a young man's fancy turns to other things.... That is why I went and bought a 'city bike', a mountain bike for softies. It has the customary eighteen gears and flashy handle bars and big fat tyres (which are very good over tram lines and saves going to the depot each time to get out). Unlike a mountain bike, it has mudguards, a stand, dynamo and lights and a carrier on the back for shopping, crates of beer, skis, firewood, etc.

Cycling is regarded in a very different light in Switzerland than in Britain. It is the greenest form of transport and is given priority and special consideration in Swiss cities that hate cars. There are many cycle lanes. Some go the wrong way up one-way streets. I have watched frustrated in my car as cyclists flout all the rules and travel through Zurich at twice the speed of cars. Now, with a bike, I can do the same. I have cycled through red lights, ridden over pavements, cycled where only trams go. I never realised how hilly Zurich is. I can get into the centre in ten minutes without pedalling most of the way. But coming back is another matter.

It is not quite as easy as just going out and buying a bike. All bikes in

Switzerland have to be registered and insured. Each cycle must have a little red number plate showing a valid insurance sticker. This requires a visit to a police station, community office or post office. For a charge of about five francs I am fully enrolled. As the bike frame number is required for registration, I thought I had to buy the bike first and to Regula's horror I rode it home without it being registered. It still worked even so. Regula has bought a bike as well, a classic lady's cycle for a classic lady. We are both somewhat saddle sore from the first few days' cycling. I have a cycle rack for the car roof so that we can soon take our bikes out into the country for long rides (once we have toughened up certain anatomical parts).

MARCH 30th:

My teaching is developing quite well and quickly at St. Addanuf. The first school, Look & Learn, is slowly going nowhere. The only people going places are the staff, who leave. They still have enough money to pay me, but the number of lessons remains constant at about five to eight a week. They were hoping to have increased their business by now, but do not appear to have succeeded. I know what the overheads of a business can be and they are not getting the income to make it a long-term, viable proposition.

APRIL 2nd:

Two weeks of mild temperatures bring the ski season to a sloppy end and we put away our skis and oil our bicycles in expectation of a new life in the cycle lane.

APRIL 14th – 21st:

Easter saw us back in England for the first time in nine months. This was the longest time I had spent away from my country. Within minutes of being driven by my parents from Heathrow Airport, it was as though I had never been gone. It was a typical English April day: windy, with clouds racing across a deep blue sky. I know the route from the airport well and driving on the 'wrong side' of the road, the houses, the buildings and the countryside did not seem foreign at all. But I had forgotten how much traffic there is, even on a Saturday in April.

It was a strange luxury to have everyone in the street and shops speaking English without difficulty, well with not too much difficulty. My sister, Angie, asked me what was the most difficult thing to teach about English. I replied that I thought the present tense is the hardest. It comes within the first few lessons and we have two. She looked blankly. Angie is an intelligent woman and a practising solicitor, but it had never occurred to her that we have two forms of the present tense in English ('I go' and 'I am going'). The reason she did not realise this was that she, like all native English-speakers, was never taught this because she already knew it before she started school. I listened to my three-year-old niece and she uses (and is using) both present tenses correctly and without difficulty. Swiss-German speaking children in Switzerland must learn High German when they start school, the British have no such disadvantage.

There is an earnest purpose in the way the Swiss go about their day which is missing in provincial England. The British are less concerned with how they look and how tidy things are about them. They are more relaxed and easy-going than the Swiss. The British do not work as hard and they are poorer for it. Not that money is everything, but the number-one worry of the average Briton is money, or rather the lack of it. However, the British do not seem to be too interested in doing much about it. It is no joke that the Swiss problem is not one of earning money, but their dilemma is finding the time to spend it. The British have the time, but not enough money. The welfare state's featherbed has left the British nation relaxed to the point of lethargy.

The difference between the British and Swiss ways of life is reflected in their respective railways. Some years ago, when we still lived in England, Regula's brother, Andreas, came over for a weekend conference in London. He phoned us to say he had Sunday free. We arranged to meet him at Southampton station.

According to the British Rail timetable, we would have had two-and-a-half hours together before he caught the train back. We arrived at the station, but there was no train. Due to maintenance work on the line, the train was two hours late.

Regula was disappointed, Andreas, when he eventually arrived, was confused and I was seething. Nor could we send him back to London by train in time to catch his plane back to Zurich, because there was a further two-hour delay on the return journey. As soon as we met him, we had to take him back by car directly from Southampton station to London.

I complained to British Rail, who refunded the return half of Andreas's ticket. They pointed out their timetable states in small print that Sunday travellers should check by phone first as disruptions often occur.

Little wonder the British use their cars so much. Sunday is a busy day on the Swiss railways. Extra trains run over Christmas in Switzerland, while British Rail closes down for two days.

In Switzerland there are timetables supported by a rule book, which in turn is backed up by liberal amounts of paperwork. The Swiss follow their system and everything works wonderfully. Naturally, if you hate rules, regulations and paperwork, then you have a problem. If you ride in a Swiss cable car, take a look at the man who is in there with you 'driving' it. Does he marvel at the scenery? No, he does not have time. He is busily filling in the time, date, number of passengers and untold other information on his forms, ensuring everything works perfectly.

There are times when the British lack of efficiency and lack of bureaucracy is wonderful. Some English friends spent a holiday in Switzerland and I drove them to Zurich airport for their flight back. At the Zurich passport-check they discovered their passports were still in the hotel safe. My two friends had to sign a form indemnifying the Swiss authorities in the event they were refused entry into the UK. At London airport they anxiously approached the immigration officer at the UK passport-check. They expected the worst as they explained their predicament to the officer who smiled and said "You won't do that again in a hurry, will you?" And that was all he said. They were waved past without further enquiries.

British cuisine has earned itself a frightful reputation. Mostly this is unjustified, but a glance round the spaciously wide aisles of a British supermarket reveals that what appears on the British dinner table differs significantly from that of Switzerland. The British have taken frozen food to their hearts. Much more space is devoted to frozen food than in Swiss supermarkets. In Britain there are now supermarkets selling only frozen food. Shopping by car once a week, or even once a month, is much favoured by the British, whereas many Swiss shop nearly every day.

The Swiss eat six times more chocolate per head than the Brits. The British counter this with their consumption of crisps, the British name for what the rest of the world calls potato chips. Swiss supermarkets devote considerable shelf space to their superior chocolate. In Britain chocolate is mainly for kids and metres of shelving are required to display the wide and exotic varieties of crisps – flavours that include sweet and sour pork, prawn cocktail, roast beef and curry.

Curry, not in the form of crisps, is something that I realise I had missed in Switzerland. In the UK Indian meals are inexpensive and available in every town and village. We topped up with a few 'Indians' while in England. I have yet to come across an Indian restaurant in Switzerland.

We bought another electric kettle while we were in England. A state-of-the-art cordless model with filter and water-gauge. I cannot understand why automatic electric kettles are not more popular in Switzerland. Most Swiss still make coffee and tea by boiling a pan of water, very old-fashioned and potentially dangerous. But the method works – so they say "why change?"

Something very odd happened to me while we were buying the kettle in an electric kettle super-store. (Every product that sells in worthwhile quantities is sold in its own super-store in Britain.) As I looked around the store, I kept seeing mistakes. Some quite serious. A drawing on the back of an accessory pack containing a TV-aerial socket showed how it should be wired up to the mains electricity. The results could be fatal. My mind has become Swiss-tuned and can spot British sloppiness a mile off (well, a kilometre at least). I pointed this error out to the management. They were surprised and appeared grateful, but I don't expect anything will change.

It was a luxury to buy English newspapers at reasonable prices again. The Swiss papers keep their national, cantonal and local news for the inside pages. The British papers are just the opposite. Having wrung out every possible scrap of British news, they reluctantly turn to foreign news by about page fifteen.

British humour has a reputation and it is true that the British laugh a lot. Presumably in the hope that this will help to maintain their reputation. I did enjoy the ease with which the British smile. In Zurich, the British tourists can often be heard on the trams because they are the only ones laughing. However, I have not found any differences between what the Swiss and the British laugh at. The British look for humour in everything, the Swiss are brought up not to expect it. My Swiss students find out in the first few minutes of the first lesson that they are allowed to laugh, and from then on they do it as easily as any Brit.

Our time in England passed all too quickly. The flight back was on the Saturday after Easter and I have never seen Heathrow so busy. It was like a proverbial cattle market. The plane was full and we sat on either side of the gangway, the only seats available on the very large and quite quiet airbus.

I sat next to a little girl who was travelling with her mother. The girl took a great deal of interest in what was going on around her on the plane. We soon got talking. She was a forward child and she explained, as she pointed to the air hostess running up and down the plane with our meals, that she too wanted to be an air hostess when she grew up. Then in the same breath, she turned to me and asked me what I wanted to be when I grew up. I paused for a moment to think and then replied that I wasn't sure.

APRIL 23rd:

Today was another one of those odd Zurich half-day holidays where offices and shops are open in the morning, but not the afternoon. This time it was because of *Sächsilüüte* (pro. Sax-ee-lootah). This literally means 'six o'clock ringing'. The local guilds have a large and elaborate parade through Zurich. They all dress up in historical costumes, some riding horses, accompanied by marching bands. This goes on for a couple of hours. The procession ends at a large bonfire with a model of a snowman on top.

The snowman's head is filled, not with silly ideas, or even thoughts of next winter, but a generous charge of explosives. So when the flames reach his head, the snowman is blown to pieces. The time between lighting the fire and the snowman losing his head is supposed to indicate how good the summer will be. This year the time was quite short, so we should have a good summer (yes please). The whole festival dates back to at least the early 1800s and is to celebrate the end of winter. We all might be happy at the thought of balmy summer days ahead. But not the Zurich guildsmen. They celebrate the longer days because they can now work past six in the evening and make more money than in the winter.

APRIL 25th:

Our visit to England helped us realise that we made the right decision to move to Switzerland. It was not a sudden realisation, but one that slowly built up as things fell into place and difficulties were overcome. The biggest difficulty living in Switzerland for me is the language and the attitude of some of the people. The more I get to know the Swiss and Switzerland, the more I am expected to comply with their approach to life.

The countryside with its picturesque mountains and lakes provides no difficulties for the would-be immigrant. High salaries more than compensate for the long working hours. Despite this, I have known English people who moved to Switzerland, only to return to Britain after some while. The reasons? In Switzerland they missed having a house and garden, which are outrageously expensive and for most simply not an option. They had to live in a relatively small flat with restrictions like being able to wash clothes only every two or three weeks, or not being allowed to take a bath after 10 pm and dozens of other regulations. Many a poor Brit cannot take living with so many rules.

There are other problems too. It seems to me that many Swiss are little policemen at heart and do not hesitate to correct others they think are falling out of line. An English friend of mine was staying with his in-laws in Lucerne, a

Catholic town. Nothing much was happening on Sunday morning so he decided to wash his father-in-law's car. No sooner had he started with a bucket of hot water and sponge than a neighbour came out and told him that it was forbidden to wash cars on Sundays.

Another English friend, who has lived in Zug for nearly twenty years, was on her way out to the shops in her car. She was due to pick up a friend and was in a hurry. It was also the day that the dustmen came and she took her plastic bag of domestic rubbish down directly into the underground car park. She put the rubbish bag in the boot, with the view of dropping it by her gate as she went out. In her haste she forgot. It was only as she came to put some things in the boot when she collected her friend that she remembered it. She removed the bag and put it on a pile of similar bags near to her friend's flat. A woman stared at her from an upstairs window as she did this, but my friend did not think too much about it at the time. She left the bag and drove off.

A few days later the postman rang the doorbell. He had a large Remy Martin Champagne gift box in his arms for her. It was, however, suspiciously light. When she opened it, she found that it contained that same rubbish bag. It also contained a letter advising her that when she had rubbish, it should be left outside her own premises, not anyone else's. The sender of the parcel must have opened the bag of rubbish and found an envelope with my friend's address on it. An extreme example to illustrate a certain mentality that exists in a minority of Swiss.

I encountered the Swiss police attitude when I went shopping once. I parked my car in the shop's parking bay, did my shopping and returned with my purchases in a shopping trolley. I filled the boot, closed it and pushed the trolley to the edge of the bay. The shop was round the corner and it was a nuisance to walk it back and trolleys are often left there. An elderly man stopped to watch me. When he saw that I was not going to return the trolley to the shop he started to shout over to me, telling me to take the trolley back. I climbed in my car and shouted to him in English, asking where his uniform was. As I drove off, I could see he was writing down my car number. I did not hear anything further, but I have no doubt that a shopping trolley offence can be serious.

These three incidents have one thing in common. In each case a car with a Swiss registration was involved. Thus it was assumed by the respective 'police-men' that those committing these horrendous crimes against Switzerland, were Swiss. Had the cars been British registered and it clear that the occupants were tourists, then the scenes would have been very different. I could imagine that the man would have taken my trolley back himself with a cheery wave. The face at the window would have smiled at my friend as she deposited her rubbish. The Lucerne neighbour could well have offered to help wash an English car.

The Swiss do not like foreigners particularly, especially those who come to live in their country. But they need them and they tolerate them. Tourists, although foreigners, hold quite a different position in Swiss society. Tourists, especially English-speaking ones, are liked very much and are allowed to do whatever they like. If they come by car, they can flout the traffic laws and drive in the wrong lanes and park where they like without difficulties. They do not need to speak a word of any language the Swiss speak, they just merrily speak their own tongue and the Swiss seem able to communicate in whatever language is needed. The Swiss love them for two reasons. Firstly, tourists bring a lot of money and the Swiss provide numerous ways for them to part with it. And secondly, and just as important, after tourists have been relieved of their money, they leave Switzerland and disappear back to their own country, hopefully to get more money and come back another day. Tourists do not stay and that is what endears them to the Swiss.

TOURIST PRIMITIVE   THE MISSING TOURIST   TOURIST ERECTUS   TOURIST SAPIENS

You can easily spot tourists in Zurich. While the *Zürcher* (which is what they call themselves rather illogically, instead of *Züricher*) are clad in the latest expensive fashions with a profusion of leather and fur, the tourist is a dowdy bird by their side. In winter the tourists wear bulging his-and-her ski anoraks under their cameras and video cameras as they tread Zurich's highly fashionable Bahnhofstrasse with trainers (not Swinglish) on their feet. The American tourist, who by the way is by far the most interesting and distinctive of the breed, will often be found in garish tartan trousers or occasionally topping the whole look with a cowboy hat. In the summer, tourists can be seen wearing shorts, as they mingle with the intense shoppers. Sometimes, and this is a British speciality, he only wears shorts and no shirt, but, as always, the obligatory camera.

Far be it from me to suggest that I would like to be regarded as one of these tourists. No, I feel that there is some middle road between being an anorak-and-trainers tourist and becoming a fully fledged member of the Swiss self-police force. When I try to speak German to people in shops and restaurants, I meet with varying degrees of success. By speaking German with an accent, I am immediately branded as a foreigner, as opposed to a tourist, and placed at the bottom of the list, with service to match. If I open up in English then I am playing on my home ground which gives me a substantial advantage. It is assumed that I am a tourist and suddenly I am top of the list.

I am developing a philosophy for survival in Switzerland, which necessitates that I remain forever what most people are for only two or three weeks of the year. Not a tourist with camera, anorak and trainers, but a tourist at heart, being ever surprised and fascinated by things new and different from one's own land. Only seeing the pleasant gloss of life and not the complications that make that pleasant life possible. I can never be Swiss at heart, but I think I can have a very nice life here as a kind of 'perpetual tourist'.

APRIL 26th:

Regula has secured a new job, which she will be starting after working out her notice. She will be working for the boss of a small company that is in the 'mergers and acquisitions' business. A sort of estate agent for companies. She will now be working 80%, quite a popular idea in Switzerland and very popular with us. We will both now have Fridays off together and have more time to be tourists.

APRIL 27th – MAY 2nd:

We managed to take a long weekend in the Ticino – the Italian part of Switzerland. It is where people from the Zurich area are always sloping off to and singing the praises of, so I had to see it. It was the first time I had been there and I was impressed. We left when the weather in Zurich was cool and cloudy. We choked our way through the fumy seventeen-kilometre-long St Gotthard tunnel, the main route through the Alps, and found ourselves in a different world. It was sunny and warm on the south side of the Alps. The vegetation is quite different there. Instead of fir trees all neatly planted and little green alpine fields, the vegetation is lush and wild. Chestnut trees were in bloom and, by the lakes, there are palm trees. Steep-roofed chalets are gone and replaced by a very Italian/Mediterranean style of architecture.

By lunch time we reached Lago Maggiore and Locarno. We stopped at a little restaurant overlooking the lake. It was very strange to be able to eat lunch outside in summer temperatures having had breakfast the same morning inside in a cool and cloudy Zurich. We went to see the place they named after our car – no not Bangor, but Ascona. We ended up in a little village called Ronco. (There is nowhere called K-Tel though.)

Ronco is a small village of luxury villas and old houses perched on a very steep hillside with views of the lake and mountains. The streets of the village are only about 1.5 metres (5ft) wide and the roofs of the buildings nearly touch each other. There is no room for cars there.

We found the *Ristorante della Posta*, a small but quite luxurious restaurant that is also a hotel with just four bedrooms. The language is Italian, the plumbing Swiss and the food superb. We ate breakfast and dinner on their open-air terrace dining room, while swallows flew above and palms, lemon trees and exotic flowers bloomed all around. We could look out over the still waters of the lake to the snow-covered peaks beyond.

The next day we went south to Morcote (pro. more-coat-eh) on Lake Lugano, described in the local tourist brochure as "the pearl of Ticino." This is an old village of churches and monasteries hanging on to the precarious slopes that rise directly up from the lake. The weather was perfect, not a cloud in the sky, the lake was like glass and the air was crystal clear, giving fantastic views.

We parked the car and started to walk up the four hundred steps to the tall tower of the church of Santa Maria del Sasso. We intended this to be just a short stop of about twenty minutes and left our walking shoes in the car. On the way up, we were quite alone. The still air, subtropical vegetation and extravagant architecture combined to produce a surreal atmosphere. It reminded me of Portmeirion in Wales, where they filmed the TV series "The Prisoner." Portmeirion is, however, only a copy of somewhere like Morcote.

We went higher to get a better view and take some pictures. One thing led to another and we found ourselves on a major climb, Regula in her shopping shoes and me in my Gucci loafers pressing on ever upward. About two hours after we had left the car to have a look at Morcote, we found ourselves in a restaurant eating a large lunch near the top of the mountain, way above the village. But it was worth it.

The car was so hot when we got back that not only was the boot full of melted chocolate and steaming walking boots, but the adhesive holding the thermometer to the outside of the windscreen had gone soft. The thermometer had slid down the screen like some big black snail with a speedometer in its back, leaving a hard sticky trail. Then it had cooled down and I was unable to budge it. Fortunately I didn't need the wipers.

The next day it was hot again and I could slide the thermometer back up to its home. We drove up various valleys and spent the third night in a very desolate and lonely village right at the top end of a valley. It was much cooler with wedges of dirty old snow still lying about. Spring was just starting there at 1400 metres (4500ft), whereas summer was in full swing down by the lakes.

The village, called Campo, was once a thriving community of 400 people who made their living by smuggling goods over the pass into Italy. This lasted for hundreds of years and finally died out in the 1950s when the falling value of the Italian lira made it uneconomical. (It is much the same story with the British pound and the so-called duty-free shop at Heathrow.) Smuggling says much about the differences between the British and the Swiss. Both nations did it, but while the Swiss smuggled stuff out, the British smuggled booty into their country.

We found what seemed to be one of the only occupied buildings left, which typically for Switzerland was a restaurant. They also had rooms to let. Although these were clean, it was fairly cold as there was no heating. We could warm our room a bit by opening the windows. There was no running water in the room. One's bodily functions were catered for by a large white potty in the bedside table. We were the only guests and a meal was cooked for us in the evening and a very good breakfast of salami and fried eggs the next morning. The restaurant was run by a former optician who had seen his future away from the Zurich rat-race and was trying to make a go of things up there. The locals from the village had all gone to Zurich to do much the same thing.

It is no wonder that half of the people who live and work in the north of Switzerland nip over, or through, the Alps at every opportunity to visit the Ticino. It is enormously popular and with very good reason. It has a kind climate and a dreamy blend of the Mediterranean and all the quality and cleanliness of Switzerland.

MAY 5th:

Zurich has a free daily newspaper. It is impressive to those of us used to the free advertising-crammed fodder-for-the-paper-collection free papers that are thrust through British letter boxes. The Zurich one has much less advertising (and so probably runs at a loss), contains TV programmes and even some news. I have never been able to get up early enough to see it being delivered. Even a 5.30 am start once found me first picking up the papers off the step.

A recent news item in the paper reported that the Zurich police have just bought thirty city bikes. (Do English bobbies still ride bikes? – I think it is too dangerous.) The Zurich police reckon bikes are faster than police cars with blue lights and horns, which is a good epithet (or should it be epitaph) to the city. It shows exactly how the car is treated, hindered by continuous red lights. The bikes do not, however, have blue lights and I presume the police have to shout "doo dah" themselves.

MAY 6th:

I am getting tired of hearing where my students go for their holidays. (I say students, they are adults.) I gave a lesson based on last year's holidays (the irregular past: go/went, eat/ate, drink/drank, hangover/hungover). I asked the class where they went last year. I got Bali a number of times, Australia, Canada, Zimbabwe, and all the exotic spots under the sun. Someone had even been to the North Pole, and in summer you can't get more under the sun than that.

MAY 7th:

Regula has started her new job. It and her old job are like chalk and cheese. The work is more interesting, but not a stress and her boss is very nice. She starts at a very leisurely 9 am. We still get up before seven and mornings seem as mad a rush as ever. The office is a little further away than the last and it takes her about twenty-five minutes by tram.

MAY 21st:

The weather is warmer. I have been going to work each day on my bike in only shirt sleeves (yeah, yeah and trousers too). The temperature of the Zürisee (the lake), which is in the paper each day, is quite high for this early in the year at 20°C (nearly 70°F). In winter it went down to 4°C. In a very cold winter the lake can freeze. By August it is usually a very comfortable 25°C. What they do not tell you is that as there is no tide to stir it up, it is only the top half metre that reaches this temperature. Below it is much colder – so one must swim very horizontally.

We have been showered with bank holidays since we have been here, what with *Knabenschiessen* (boys shooting) and *Sächsilüüte*, and this does not seem to subside with the passing seasons. After the May 1st holiday (actually held on May 1st, what a novelty), this week we have *Auffahrt* (pro 'oofert' in Swiss-German), that is Ascension Day. *Pfingstmontag* (Whit Monday) follows in early June.

There are, however, two problems with all these bank holidays. When I do not teach, I do not get paid and it always seems to rain on these days. It is very noticeable here how warm it stays in the evening after a warm day. There is usually little or no wind in Swiss evenings and no big mass of cold sea surrounding us and cooling us down again quickly like in the British Isles.

JUNE 1st:

For the last eight years foreign workers have been digging like moles under Zurich – no, not to escape, but to build the new *S-Bahn* (*Schnellbahn* = Fast Train or Railway) which opened amid great ballyhoo. As you look out from Zurich to the lake on the left-hand side there is a long tree-covered hill, the Züriberg (a glacial lateral moraine in fact). Behind this are a number of towns, which have grown over the years as they became dormitory towns for Zurich. Until now, to commute has meant coming round the hill by train and approaching Zurich from the back. This takes about forty-five minutes.

Now a new double-decker train goes straight through the hill and takes a mere seven minutes. At the same time they have taken the opportunity to link up two other Zurich stations which were previously unconnected. This has been done deep beneath the city streets and the river. With one ticket it is now possible to use every form of public transport in the Canton. The *S-Bahn* does not affect us, except that our monthly ticket is going up to help pay for it. It will be better when all the digging is over. Knowing Zurich, I am sure they will start digging up something else immediately.

JUNE 7th:

We have at last been to the Zurich 'street traffic office' to get our Swiss driving licences before a year is over and before driving tests are required. It was all quite painless. Having got my brother-in-law, the doctor, to write a statement confirming that I could see, and having filled in the appropriate forms, the licences will be sent to us in due course, complete with photographs and a bill for Sfr 70 each. It is against the law to drive without having your licence with you and subject to a Sfr 20 instant fine. Since the Swiss ones take some days to prepare, we get to keep our British licences as well.

JUNE 11th:

We went to hear Regula's father's orchestra again so I could see someone playing the faggot. The faggot was in such high esteem that no less than Wolfgang Amadeus Mozart actually wrote a concert for it. I am not sure if Mozart played one, ate one or was one... All right, *Fagott* is German for bassoon, but it had you going there for a moment. Sadly, I was the only one in the audience that found this the slightest bit amusing.

JUNE 16th:

The Swiss continue to expose their soul over European unity. They have endless debates on what they should do. What they would really like is to have all the advantages of the Community, such as larger markets, no tariffs and free movement of goods – while not actually joining it. Keeping their neutrality would not be a problem, but the Swiss do not want to join NATO or the United Nations. They want to keep their own laws on everything from marriage to the

Switzerland sails against the wind.

size of lorries allowed on the roads and to control the numbers of foreign workers coming into the country. Somehow the most exclusive club in Europe has managed to end up with the highest percentage of foreigners in Europe (about 18%). The Swiss fear that the highest wages and the lowest unemployment in Europe would mean that people would get crushed in the rush to come here.

The British have long pursued a have-your-cake-and-eat-it-too policy towards the EU, negotiating special deals for themselves. Switzerland would like the same – a special membership with none of the disadvantages of conforming to pan-European standards and increased bureaucracy. I feel the Swiss have nothing to fear from remaining an island in the middle of Europe. Measured on an income per capita basis, they are the most successful country in Europe. The cautious and conservative Swiss nature may be the reason for their continued success and this nature now causes this national soul searching. I see no reason why the Swiss should not continue to exist as prosperously as ever in the midst of a uniting Europe. Prosperity is the keyword. The real fear of the Swiss is that by not joining the rest of Europe, they could lose some of it.

Speaking of prosperity, the postman rang the door bell. He held a small brown envelope in his hand bearing the return address of my sister, Angie, in England on one side and a 20 p stamp on the other. One of the many anomalies in the European Union is that postage is the same throughout the community. Why is this an anomaly? Well, dear little Switzerland is a nonmember and so postage from the UK to Switzerland is actually higher than from the UK to EU member Greece, even though the latter is much further away. The Swiss postman was not prepared to release the letter until I gave him 60 *Rappen.* Now I can neither send nor receive letters without the correct postage. The question is, how come these letters can get out of the UK in the first place? Still, that is not something for us tourists to worry about.

JUNE 25th:
We left a house behind in England. It wouldn't fit in the van. Our house is theoretically for sale, but the property market seems to have given up the ghost. I have been in regular and sometimes vigorous correspondence with my local council in England on the thorny subject of the Community Charge, better known as the wretched poll tax. Essentially they want to levy this new tax on our empty house, which is quite poll-less. Poll being old English for the head, or the bit where the hair grows, or used to grow.

Under this inappropriately named Community Charge, for I am no longer a member of that community, we must pay as though two people lived in our empty house. In cash terms this is £714.42 (Sfr 1570) per year. We do not use the dustbins, visit the library, wear down the roads, send children to the local school, or even flush the toilet, but we are expected to pay towards all these. The irony is that if one person lived in our house and thus was able to use the council's facilities, the charge would be half the amount they want for it being empty. It was my hope that this new poll tax would be fairer than the previous rating system. Fat chance.

I wrote a series of letters to the council in England, pointing out the anomaly of this new 'fairer system'. I asked if we could expect this reverse-logic policy to be applied to other enterprises of the council, such as the buses and car parks. Would we soon see a car park where the longer you stayed there the cheaper it became? And a bus fare structure that charged more for short journeys than for long ones? Better still, would the council soon pay their staff on the principle that the more senior they are, the less they are paid? Their replies, which always took about five to six weeks minimum and reflected the volume of queries this tax was generating, were cool and couched in legal jargon. The arguments rumbled on, but I got nowhere.

The poll tax affair got a fair amount of press and TV coverage in Switzerland and many students asked me about it. You can imagine that I put in some really good PR for the tax. In the end I gave up and paid up, which, it seems, is more than millions of others did. It did however make some of the Swiss bureaucracy suddenly seem not so bad after all.

JUNE 27th:

I searched for something to bring a smile to my face and found it in an unlikely source. When paying the bills at the end of the month through my bank, I noticed there is provision on the form for a personal reference of up to twenty-five words. This reference then appears on my bank statement in addition to the name of the payee. At first I wrote rather mundane things like "February Payments" and "Electric Bill". But when I got my statement these seemed rather dull and too business like. So now I enter more light-hearted comments, such as "Jolly Holidays", when paying for our holiday. Or "It's Only Money" and "Isn't Banking Fun?" or "Only 199 days to Xmas". I find this very satisfying, particularly as this is entered into the bank's computer and it appears every time I look at my account on the screen at one of the Bancomat cash points. I have started writing messages for the poor person who keys all this stuff into the bank's computer, like: "Keep on Bankin" and "Got any samples?" It cheers up a dreary day's shopping like nothing else. I just pop my card in the slot and the little screen shows all my daft comments. Better still, I can push a button and the silly machine prints my statement with them on.

JUNE 29th:

With our impending holiday in Greece in mind, four weeks ago I embarked upon a generally useless, but nevertheless obligatory tradition for me in the pre-holiday weeks – dieting. I am not too fat. I could just do with shaping up and shedding a bit of winter flab to enable me to fit into the same swimming trunks I wore five years ago. More important, it would stop Regula complaining about me eating too much on holiday. I have tried all sorts of diets with varying degrees of success, or to be accurate, varying degrees of failure. I was once recommended a banana diet. One can eat as many bananas as one wants, but nothing else. The problem was that the knuckles of the person who recommended it to me now drag on the ground as he walks.

I am trying a 'psychological' diet, where I just think thin for a month. This means I reach for the low-cal yogurt instead of regula(r). (I've been trying to work that joke in since the first page.) I try to resist the extra helpings at meals and exercise a bit more. The result is that over the last four weeks I have lost two kilos. Unfortunately, I cannot see where from.

Speaking of diets, I saw an interview on TV with a couple of Americans who say that no diet works, as only a complete and permanent change of eating habits will result in permanent weight loss. They have written a best-selling book applauding the wonders of complete vegetarianism – veganism. That means not even drinking milk or eating dairy products or any other animal produce. They said that it would save the world and stop the greenhouse effect too. In the US, 16 million animals *a day* are slaughtered for food. This requires incredible amounts of space to rear the cattle, untold amounts of energy, food for the animals, you name it. Two million butchers killing eight animals each a day, for example. But what about the unemployment veganism would create? I find it a bit extreme and this was supported by the appearance of the vegan couple on TV who looked like a pair of laughing skulls.

JUNE 30th:

Having already gone east on my bike, I tried cycling northwards. There is a route specially for bikes to the north of Zurich along the river Glatt. I picked up the cycle route next to the airport and from then on it was all tarred track. Without a car in sight, I followed the river through manicured fields and tidy woods. With a sandwich lunch, I kept on pedalling, the idea being that I could reach the German border.

Two hours later the little road led over a hill to a large power generating station and a ten-metre high dam that spanned a fast flowing river. I had reached the Rhine. On the other side I could see a yellow, red and black flag flying and a sign inscribed 'Bundesrepublik Deutschland'. There was a paved footpath over the top of the dam that ran from a little office and an iron gate under a Swiss flag. I pushed my bike up to the office, but nobody was there. The gate was open. I pushed my bike past and on over the dam above the roaring waters of the Rhine.

At the German side there was also an office, this too was unmanned. I kept on pushing my bike. The path rose up and away from the river and I started to cycle again. This side of the river looked just like the other. I followed the path round a field and after about three kilometres, I came to a little village. All the cars had German number plates, the post box had a curious horn symbol on it. The shop windows of the village displayed unfamiliar products priced in German marks.

My mind raced: this was the fatherland and I was just minutes from the Swiss border and freedom. The weeks of planning, the sleepless nights as we dug the tunnel under Gerry's nose. The jumping horse hid the earth that we took from the tunnel. The false papers so cleverly forged by Ginger. I had even shaved off the old handlebar moustache as part of my disguise as a Bavarian tourist who got lost on a cycling holiday near the Swiss border. The words that I heard when I first entered our stalag still rang in my ears: "For you Tommy ze var is over".

Over indeed! It was just up to me and my trusty cycle now. Three short kilometres and I would be on my way back to Blighty. And I had a score to settle with Gerry...

I could not help thinking along those lines as I cycled back from the village towards the Swiss border again. Completely alone and unchallenged, I crossed back over what was at one time a heavily guarded and barbed-wire strewn frontier. In a way I was rather hoping that I might have to make a heroic dive into the foaming waters to make one last hopeless bid for freedom. Instead I stopped on a grassy bank and ate my sandwiches.

JULY 2nd:

We spent a very pleasant Sunday with Regula's other brother, Hannes, and his family. It was the confirmation of their daughter, Ursina, who is also Regula's goddaughter. The church was nice enough. Somewhat austere in typical Swiss fashion, built in heavy stone, but thankfully not a modern concrete bunker. Other than a large and elaborate church-organ, there were no crosses or any other signs of religious decorations. The place was packed. Thirty-five fifteen and sixteen-year-olds were being confirmed, each with various parents, godparents etc. in attendance. The minister was young and notorious as somewhat of an evangelical. He was also very keen on using a radio microphone, but kept forgetting to pull out the aerial.

The thirty-five confirmees ran the service themselves. Regula thought the service, if that is the right word, was "disappointing." Her mother did not understand most of it and I have never seen anything like it. Two girls opened the service with a prayer. Ursina played '*Für Elise*' on the piano (you know – "dee da, dee da, dee da dee dee da").

From then on it was downhill all the way. Pop and disco music was played as various scenes from modern life were acted out. It became very confused and a bit of a shambles. The scene demonstrating that drugs and drinking were bad, seemed to be encouraging it as far as I could make out. In their modern theology, the devil appeared to be the ozone hole and his followers cut down the rain forests while the powers of good were represented by Martin Luther King Jr. There was no communion and it all ended in hand shakes for the thirty-five confirmees, a collection in aid of the World Wildlife Fund and then they all piled out of the door for a cigarette. Regula does, however, stress that this was not a usual Swiss Protestant confirmation service.

JULY 3rd:

An important anniversary has come around. No, not our wedding anniversary, we both forgot that again. Today is the day that twelve months ago we officially moved to Switzerland. It is a date I cannot forget, as I have had to put it on so many forms since.

JULY 13th – 20th:

This summer we have wised up. Instead of trying to look for jobs while everyone is on holiday, we joined the hordes and headed for the Greek Isle of Lesbos. It is a relatively undeveloped island. The first charter flight there was only nine years ago and the airport has one building, one runway and only one plane, ours. By contrast nine years ago in Corfu they were extending the runway to take jumbos and laying a pipeline to the mainland to pump beer directly to all the island's tavernas. Our Lesbos hotel overlooked a little working fishing harbour. And the fishermen seemed to do just that – work little. Our room was on the top floor with a perfect view over the harbour. Charming and always interesting, but rather noisy, with lots of boat noises and coughing in the early morning. At night the whole place became one great big outdoor restaurant with the nearly continuous sound of corks being pulled out of bottles.

If you ever want a stray cat, Lesbos is the place to go. They have more cats than people there. Every restaurant had its own set of strays that would beg at the tables each night.

The package holiday was run by a Swiss company. It was very like a British package holiday with a few notable exceptions. As Switzerland is halfway to the Mediterranean resorts, flights are shorter. They do not enter the dreaded French air-traffic controllers' space, with its associated delays, so are on time. The industry is smaller, but it is also slightly profitable. How does it do that? The answer is simple. They charge more for their holidays.

The British travel industry is a graveyard for tour operators. Yet they never learn and still insist on cutting prices to the bone, and beyond. Back in 1973 I went for a long winter weekend to Tunisia with the Lord Brothers travel company. The cost for three nights full board including flights and transfers at a first class hotel with a swimming pool that steamed in the February air was £23 per person. They also offered weekends in Mallorca from £9.99, cheaper than one night at a British hotel. The result: Lord Brothers went bust. As did Clarksons, who took me to Capri for a week for £28. By contrast the Swiss travel industry charges such high prices that I know of people who have flown to England and then gone on an English package holiday for two weeks to the Mediterranean from London. This was cheaper than going directly from Switzerland. But Swiss holiday companies can afford to send their customers cards at Christmas.

JULY 21st – AUGUST 1st:

As soon as we came back from Greece, I slung the windsurfer on the roof of the faithful old car and pointed it in the direction of England. It is as simple as that. You need some Frenchy francs for the autoroute tolls, petrol and enough credit card or cash for the ferry ticket. The ferry companies, in contrast to the British package-holiday industry have always known how to charge. There is nothing else to it, but to follow the signs for Basle, Strasbourg, Reims, Calais (preferably in that order). There are other routes, like through Belgium where the motorways are free. Either way, the journey takes about eight very boring hours behind the wheel. I am inclined to report that all went like clockwork, but that is an unfortunate reference in relation to that journey. I stopped at an autoroute rest area to put some sun-tan cream on my burning left arm which caught the sun as I drove. I had lost my own watch and Regula kindly loaned me hers, which I took off and put on the roof of the car as I applied the cream. Somehow I forgot to put the watch on again. The watch was last seen in my rear view mirror disappearing under the wheels of a juggernaut as I rejoined the autoroute.

It was very strange to arrive in England in a foreign car. The lady at the customs leaned through the window, smiled nervously and then mouthed very clearly as though I did not understand a word: " H o w   l o n g   a r e   y o u   s t a y i n g   i n   E n g l a n d ?" I smartly replied "About two weeks." She was obviously very relieved and said "Oh good, you speak English! You can go." As I drove out of the docks I wondered to myself what horrible punishment Her Majesty's Customs deal out to those unfortunate enough not to speak English. But there I was, a tourist in my own country as well.

The trip was really to see my family and do a bit of windsurfing in a decent wind for a change. The return journey to Switzerland was uneventful. I got back home (oh Dr Freud, I've made one of your slips!) at 6.15 pm. As I was unloading the Tortilla Chips and SHREDDIES from the car, Regula came walking up the road back from the office. The timing was perfect. And I was back in Switzerland just in time to see another few million francs' worth of fireworks go up in smoke on August 1st, Swiss National Day.

AUGUST 6th:

August is a nice month in Switzerland. There may be no sea, but there are plenty of places to swim and the lakes and rivers have warmed up nicely by now. On the hottest days there is only one thing to do. On days when the British press would be full of tales of melting tar and buckling railway lines, we pick a lake or the river Rhine and, with a bottle of chilled wine in the cool box, set out to keep cool. The Rhine is very fast flowing and relatively fresh at about 23°C and the sport is to walk up stream, jump in and then swim, float and roll back down in the current. Certainly it is about the coolest place around. And rather strange for me, a salt-water-wave-and-tide-man, to be in a fast flowing, clear and clean fresh-water river.

AUGUST 16th – 19th:

Regula's father comes from Appenzellerland in the north-east corner of Switzerland and it does not take much encouragement to get him to go back. We went there on an excellent four days' walking holiday with him. Appenzellerland is where the Säntis mountain is. The natives are even more fiercely independent than the rest of Switzerland and this was the last area to give women the vote. Our local guide was a 40-year-old independent voting-woman. One evening we went to a concert in a tent which featured Swiss folk music, *Hudigääggeler*, (pro. Hoodee-gackela) and a bit of yodelling. To prove her independence, our guide brought her pet parrot and smoked her pipe. Not to be upstaged, the men wore large earrings and smoked their pipes upside-down.

AUGUST 21st:

One feature of Swiss life that is becoming more and more noticeable to me is 'begging letters', a computer-based and highly polished and sophisticated form of the old art of begging. Hardly a day goes by without a letter in the postbox from some cause or another who needs our donations. Often harrowing and distressing pictures are accompanied by a letter explaining how we can help relieve the situation. Sometimes we are sent colourful cards complete with envelopes, or maybe an elaborate colour brochure. All are accompanied by two PTT giro payment forms. One made out for about Sfr 15 and another blank so you can always give more. Many of these are deserving causes, but there are political parties looking for contributions and some must be very suspect organisations.

If they were addressed to me, I would throw them all away. As Regula is the Swiss and I am the tourist, her name is on the voting list and so the begging letters are addressed to her. This means she meticulously collects fifteen or twenty a month. At the end of the month we have a big debate over which should be paid and which should be thrown out. Presumably many people pay, or it would not be worth sending out these begging letters. Like the other Swiss form of begging – busking, it is well supported.

Recently a much more direct and old-fashioned form of begging has developed in Zurich's streets whereby tramps, alcoholics and the blossoming population of drug addicts sit next to a cardboard box with a suitable message on it. When translated these read along the lines of 'saving for fare to Sydney' or 'drink problem to support' and the like. There is usually a half-empty bottle of wine nearby to indicate to would-be donors that their funds are soon put to use. Eventually the police move them on. This is a feature of all big cities these days. London is no different with its homeless who sleep rough each night.

Zurich council embarked a few years ago on a unique policy towards drug addicts and, although drug taking is illegal, they decided to hand out free needles to prevent the spread of AIDS. The council are now reaping the rewards of this policy in the form of begging, petty crime and the fact that Zurich has become a Mecca for drug addicts from other areas, not to mention other countries. The drug addicts are all restricted to one area, whether by design or not I do not know, but this has meant that a park in Zurich (now known as 'Needle Park') is a no-go area. My gripe is that, while I had such a palaver getting into my wife's country in order to work and pay taxes, at the same time there are drug addicts being handed out needles at the tax payers' expense.

Of all the cities in the world, probably the last place where there should be people begging in the streets is Zurich. So far begging is such a novelty for the locals that they are handing out large sums to anyone who sits in the street and asks. A local paper featured this new phenomenon and reported that beggars could double their income by writing on their cardboard boxes that they were HIV positive. They also reported that one young man earned a record Sfr 500 for one day's begging in Zurich. If English teaching should ever become too difficult, I know what else I could do.

AUGUST 30th:

It is a mystery why so many people smoke in Switzerland, far more than in Britain these days. Smoking has been banned for many years in Swiss buses and trams as well as many public places such as cinemas. However, it is very

Swiss moped rider trying a crash helmet for size.

noticeable how many people smoke in other places, especially near me in restaurants when I am eating.

Another mystery is that, although it is compulsory to wear crash helmets when riding mopeds in Switzerland, only about half the riders do. Many wear their helmets on their elbows as they ride, which must be where they keep their brains. The police stop and book offenders whenever they see them, but that does not seem to stop the habit. It is much the same with seat belts in cars. These have been compulsory for a number of years, but still only about 70% of people wear them. This figure is considerably lower in the French and Italian parts of Switzerland. In the UK over 99% of drivers and front seat passengers wear seat belts. It cut down on deaths and injuries so much that the occupants of rear seats were being injured more than front-seat ones. So the British government then made wearing seat belts in back seats compulsory too. The British would rather not be killed or maimed if at all possible. You would have thought in a strictly controlled country like Switzerland that gave the world muesli, where health and the environment are paramount, that all motorcyclists would wear helmets and every car driver and passenger would wear seat belts and nobody would smoke. But nearly the opposite is true.

My conclusion is that, as many things are tightly controlled in Switzerland, there is a feeling of infringement of personal liberty. Many people, particularly the younger ones, protest by not wearing seat belts and helmets. Much the same is true with smoking, plus perhaps the stress at work and pressures to succeed are higher in Switzerland and smoking is a safety valve.

SEPTEMBER 10th

That strange Zurich 'Boys Shooting' holiday is here again. They will have to change the name as next year it will include girls as well, whatever next?

SEPTEMBER 18th:

Autumn walking weather is back and we did a famous walk, known as the 'five lakes walk' because, by wonderful Swiss logic, it goes past five lakes. The walk is high up in an area above Wangs-Pizol, a name that causes amusement to the English speaker.

I am often puzzled at the popularity of Interlaken with British tourists. It is only a town between two lakes but there are dozens of equally interesting and beautiful places to visit in Switzerland. Could it be that it is one of the few places that can be pronounced by English-speaking tourists?

SEPTEMBER 21st:

No sooner have I found a way to have a little fun than it is stopped. My bank has issued new forms for me to pay my bills with and these no longer have any provision for writing choice comments. The bank may have stopped me putting little jokes on my statements, but life is a little poorer for it. I will not be put off so easily.

SEPTEMBER 23rd:

The Swiss went to cast their votes again. Amongst the subjects this time round was 'should Switzerland phase out atomic power stations?' There is a general unease about nuclear power, not only in Switzerland, and Chernobyl did nothing to relieve this. Only 2% of Switzerland's electricity is generated by oil and 52% by hydroelectric schemes and the balance of 46% by nuclear power. Switzerland actually exports 20% of the power it generates, doubtless the cleanest, safest and most efficient electricity in the world! Thus there is scope to cut back on production of electricity by nuclear power. The proposal is to close all the nuclear power stations by 2025 and make up the difference with power saving and alternative sources. The initiative was complicated with three levels of nuclear cutbacks proposed. The result was a suitably Swiss compromise. They voted to stop building any new nuclear powered generating stations, but only for ten years.

SEPTEMBER 25th:

Personal labour in Switzerland is expensive – doctors, dentists, plumbers, hopefully English teachers and of course hairdressers. With this in mind I had my hair cut particularly short before we first came here. But eventually I had to submit to Swiss scissors.

Swiss hairdressers like to make appointments more than they like to cut hair. Even if the shop is empty an appointment is required. I once found a hairdresser's with a notice in the window saying no appointment was necessary. Even so, I had to give my name and phone number and come back in twenty minutes.

Last week I tried a newly opened and highly fashionable unisex tonsorial boutique, with the traditional Swiss name of 'Hair Force'. The windows were full of wild photos of people being scalped at hair cutting sessions on local disco dance floors. Inside it was not dissimilar to a fairground hall of mirrors, complete with thundering disco music coming from a bank of six colour TVs mounted in the ceiling so that customers can watch while their hair is being washed. The TVs bash out nonstop rock videos from MTV (Music Television) all day. Although I was the only customer and three staff members were on duty, I had to make an appointment and come back the next day.

I asked for something a little different, but not too wild having seen the photos of the decapitations on the disco floor. I ended up with what I have spent the last thirty-five years trying to avoid. Since being a young lad, I have begged hairdressers to leave my sideboards. They are gone and my hair is now so short

Did you have any particular style in mind, Sir?

that white skin, last visible in my cradle, has been revealed. If a hairdresser had done this to me when I was fifteen, I would have come home crying. Regula looked blankly at my hair and said, "Not today, thank you," as she closed the door in my face. On the bright side, the cut should last a long time and it cost me under an hour's wages, just.

OCTOBER 6th – 13th:

We took an organised walking holiday in Cinque Terre, Italy, a very hilly and attractive coastal area on the left-hand side of Italy just at the top of the boot. Cinque Terre is pronounced 'chinkway terray' and means 'five Terrys'.

The journey there and back must rate as one of the less boring railway journeys of the world. The line goes south from Zurich, snaking its way up to the Gotthard tunnel. Often the train turns a complete spiral inside mountains to gain height. We had spectacular views of towering mountains above us and to the sides, sheer drops. After the Gotthard tunnel, we descended the warm slopes of the Ticino and its lakes. Over the border into Italy, the train presses on to the flat, fertile valley of the River Po. Then the sprawling suburbs of Milan appear;

tall blocks of faceless flats with washing hanging from nearly every window. The schedule requires some shunting about and passengers are rewarded for their patience with an excellent view of the station. Unfamiliar sights await the Swiss traveller, such as rubbish all over the tracks and filthy, rundown factories backing onto the railway. Once out of Milan, the train speeds noisily across the flat flood plain of the Po again. At last a range of dusty mountains comes into view and the train darts into a series of tunnels. We rattled into Genoa to the sight of the Italian navy just going on leave. After further shunts we were off again, this time along the coast. Every time someone pointed to the sea or a particular view, the train heard them and darted into another tunnel to block the view. The gaps between tunnels are so short that if we blinked we missed them. The technique was to keep your view fixed through the window, even through the tunnels, so as not to miss the bits in between.

Cinque Terre's wooded peaks are over 500m (1500ft) high and rise steeply from the Mediterranean. Because of the hills, Cinque Terre was cut off from the world for many years and is, by Italian standards, well-preserved and unspoilt. It consists of five fishing villages (territories or 'terre's') each precariously built on narrow river-valleys where they meet the sea. The combination of steep, wobbly wash-painted houses, tight little harbours of crystal water with terraced vineyards on the hills behind and air thick with the scent of wild herbs is intoxicating.

The first day, as we stepped from the hotel to start an interesting little walk, the heavens opened and it poured most of the day. But every cloud has a silver lining and, with bolts of lightning falling around us, we were able to give our newly purchased matching 'his and hers' walking capes the Italian torrent test. They kept the rain out well. But they also kept the primitive bodily function known to the upper classes as perspiration, well and truly in. By lunch time we were as wet inside our capes as out. Everyone was similarly soaked from the pours as well as the pores. After that, we had five successive days without a cloud in the sky.

The hotel and food were good. The food tended to be on the side of quantity rather than quality. I made a miscalculation between the calories burnt off by walking and the calories per serving of spaghetti, risotto, wine by the bucket etc. As a result, I have returned home to grace the bathroom scales at a new lifetime's best.

Now I understand why the Swiss do not wander too far beyond the Italian part of Switzerland when heading south. Italy is not cheap. Hotels, meals out and shop prices are only marginally less expensive than Switzerland. Italy is also dirty. Even in the tourist area of Cinque Terre, all household rubbish, which appears to consist of an inordinate number of washing up liquid bottles and blue plastic bags, is shoved down the nearest pretty slope. The lira is a very silly currency too. One has to carry around a quarter of a million of them just to pay for drinks during a week's stay. It is time they took off some noughts. It really is barmy to have a 1000 lire note and find that it is worth the princely sum of one Swiss franc.

On our homeward journey we saw how the *Föhn* is made. It starts in a very humid, cloudy Italy at about 26°C where it does not do much good at all and just hangs around and annoys people and makes them work even slower. But as the *Föhn* is pushed over the Alps, all the nasty bits, like moisture and fog and clouds, are wrung out over the Italians and then the Italian Swiss. By the time it rolls down the north face of the Alps, it is the warm, dry wind that everybody likes, except those poor individuals who get a headache or have traffic accidents during it.

OCTOBER 17th:

Mad cow disease is the latest craze to arrive in Switzerland from Britain. A mad cow was spotted near Bern. It was apprehended and quickly brought to its senses.

OCTOBER 21st:

We had two free tickets from Regula's father for a concert-cum-speeches do at the Zurich concert hall. The whole thing was rather long. It was in aid of the 50th anniversary of the 'Swiss Patronage to Help Poor Mountain Communities' to which Regula and her father contribute. He contributes more than she does and he got two free tickets. There was a performance of a rare concerto for alphorn and orchestra, which was very good. Our patience for sitting through the long speeches was rewarded by a free aperitif (what the Swiss call an *Apéro*). At first this seemed to be a rather mean affair with only half a dozen plates of canapes and an equal number of bottles of wine for about 500 people. But in typical Swiss style, instead of piling everything they had up high at the start for show, the caterers just kept on slowly bringing out more and more. Each time we thought it was over, out came something else to eat. In the end we had to leave or burst.

OCTOBER 28th:

A milestone has been reached. The new edition of the Zurich phone book is just out and as we are now in it, we feel as though we really have arrived. As previously predicted we are the only Biltons in the book. When we applied for the phone I did not have an entry or residents' permit. To avoid having to make a Sfr 500 deposit with the PTT, as is usual with foreigners, the phone is in Regula's name. The Swiss phone book also prints, on request, the subscribers' professions next to their names. I cannot see this working in England. There would be an inordinate amount of 'brain surgeons' and 'chicken sexers' in the British phone book.

The British can never be trusted to take anything like that seriously. Some years ago I went on a ski holiday from England. I thought it would be amusing to supply a daft photo of myself for the ski pass. When I collected my pass, I was very disappointed to find that the photo of me from my summer holidays wearing a straw hat and sunglasses with a large cocktail in hand, blended in with all the other crazy photos of the rest of the British ski party. These included crossed eyes, tongues out, half a dozen backs of heads and one man who supplied a photo taken when he was ten years old. Sadly, modern electronic tickets are dispensing with the need for photographs on ski passes.

We celebrated our recognition by the phone book with a meal at a nearby restaurant that specialises in local grub. On the 'try anything once' principle, I had a horse fillet steak for the first time (well, at least knowingly) and I must admit that it was delicious; very tender with no particular strong taste. There is quite a tradition of horse butchery in Switzerland. They are the shops with no windows, as they do not like to show off their wares too much. Perhaps this is in case someone once rode it or even backed it in the 1.30. It brings a new meaning to the expression 'I could eat a horse'.

NOVEMBER 4th:

Some years ago the normally sensible citizens of Zurich voted in a socialist city council, a coalition of reds and greens who have many ideas that smack of the British loony left. Speaking of colours, the whole of Zurich is to become a 'blue zone'. That means parking time will be controlled by a disc you place in your car window which shows when you parked. In areas, like our road, which do not already have meters, parking will be limited to one or two hours. Residents will be able to get a permit (at a price). The blue-zone system is to discourage people from bringing their cars into the town, but is of no real help to people who live here, nor will it discourage the use of cars. In fact, people may well think that as they have paid for a permit, they better get some use out of the car. It will certainly keep some customers away from the Zurich shops.

At the same time the speed limit is to be reduced to 30kph (20mph) on all roads in the whole built-up region of Zurich, except through-roads, which will remain at 50kph (30mph). This means my bike will be faster than the car. Why don't they build more bike lanes? The first blue zones are already in operation. These involve liberal use of 'sleeping policemen' (bumps intentionally built across the roads), widened pavements and assorted concrete obstacles to make driving hazardous. Many of the roads, such as the one we live in, are so narrow that it is impossible to drive more than 30kph anyway. All that has happened so far is that seven cyclists have been injured falling off their bikes when they hit the 'sleeping policemen'.

The city taxes are to go up to finance various social programmes, including giving drug addicts free syringes, which can be as many as 7000 a day in the summer when addicts come to Zurich for their holidays.

NOVEMBER 12th:

I am pleased to report that my weight has slowly subsided to its pre-Cinque Terre level. I want to lose a bit more so that I can fit into my ski suit again. It looks as though we might for once have some snow this winter. A storm which, by Swiss accounts, appears to have had its origins somewhere near Birmingham and which somehow arrived here two days late, with no indication where it had been in the meantime, has brought a good covering of early snow to the higher Alpine slopes and even given Zurich's Uetliberg a white sugaring. This was the sign we needed to do the Swiss thing and put our summer clothes away and our winter plumage on. I should put the winter tyres on the car. Even if I do not need them, with eight wheels spread around a four-wheeled car, the tyres should last twice as long.

NOVEMBER 17th

Before leaving England we had investigated the possibility of letting our house for rent, but concluded that the potential was greater for aggravation than profit. With current reports on the UK housing market indicating that we could not even give our house away, we have reconsidered. Within a month of offering the house for rent we have a tenant. The council can poll tax someone else now.

In Switzerland about 70% of people rent rather than own their homes. Property is expensive and therefore rents are also high, but landlords cannot just raise the rent because they feel they can get more money, even when a tenancy changes. The rents are all registered and can only be raised when interest rates go up, or when the property is completely refurbished, not just redecorated. An inspector has to come round to the flat and give his approval for a rent rise.

The British private rental market is very small and landlords can ask whatever rent they want. However, once on the property, tenants can be impossible to remove, even if they do not pay the rent. We hope to avoid this with our house by using an experienced agent and a fixed-term contract.

NOVEMBER 27th:

November turned out to have one or two good points after all. Last year's snow arrived about eleven months late. We woke up yesterday morning to find it had snowed in the night and there was 15 – 20 cms (6 – 8 inches) of the stuff all over Zurich.

With the temperature above freezing, it was wet and heavy snow, rather like a liberal spraying of ready-mix concrete over everything. A tree in the front garden that had resisted the ravages of umpteen British-made storms was brought to its knees by the weight of snow. Instead of everyone taking a day off work, schools closing, helicopters flying food to stranded motorists, police advising the public not to make journeys unless they were absolutely necessary and headlines like 'Phew what a Freezer!' or 'Arctic Switzerland Shivers' etc., life just went on as normal. We had to wait until 7.25 am before our little road was snow ploughed. The main road had been ploughed about every ten minutes throughout the night.

DECEMBER 2nd:

Our old friend the *Föhn* is back and we can see the snow-capped mountains very clearly from the hill near our flat. We took an afternoon stroll up the hill and bought some hot chestnuts on the way. Italians sell these all over the place from about the beginning of October onwards.

On the subject of nuts, there is a walnut tree at the end of the road and a couple of months ago Regula brought home some nuts that had fallen off it. They were very nice and sweet, much nicer than the shop bought ones. I cannot recall ever seeing walnuts growing in England. Sadly in Switzerland horse chestnuts, the conker, so highly prized by British school-boys, is ignored and left to rot with the dead leaves.

It is funny how some things are the opposite way round – like salt and pepper. The British salt cellar has just one hole, while the Swiss counterpart has a number of holes like the British pepper pot. And, you guessed it, the Swiss pepper pot has only one hole, like the British salt cellar.

This is guaranteed to cause confusion for the average tourist, but the perpetual tourist is already aware of such things. He will never stand out in a Swiss self-service restaurant by removing the contents of his tray onto the table and putting his tray on the floor like the British do. He will follow the practical Swiss and leave everything on the tray and eat off that. At the end of the meal he will not just walk away and let some menial clear up his tray at Sfr 20 per hour. He will instead take his tray with all the dirties and place it in a mobile trolley especially designed to take the trays.

The perpetual tourist will also be aware how the Swiss early-start to the day affects eating habits for the rest of the day and so will not attempt to eat between 12.00 and 1.00 pm, when all the restaurants are full. Likewise, in the evening if the perpetual tourist wants to eat out and get a seat in a restaurant without any difficulties, he will eat after 8.30 pm, when all the Swiss are in bed.

DECEMBER 10th:

The Swiss chose December as the month in which to count themselves in a census. They are going to count me as well, aren't I lucky? I just hope that nobody is missing.

DECEMBER 20th:

It snowed hard, a real Arctic storm. The postman managed to fight his way through and he rang our bell. I am wise enough by now to know this means there was a letter from England with not enough stamps on it. I played the wise guy and did not answer the bell. It is near Christmas and I was sure I could count on the postman's festive spirit to leave the letter if I were not there.

After about five minutes when I was sure he was gone I sneaked down to the postbox on the ground floor. Instead of cheery wishes from friends in England, there was an official looking form advising that a delivery requiring me to come to the post office after two that afternoon awaited my collection.

This looked important. They wanted me to bring identification. Maybe somebody was trying to send me money?

By the afternoon, the weather was even worse, but I was undeterred. I wrapped up well, pulled my cap down low and ventured out. Luckily I knew the way to the post office well because the world had been transformed into a white featureless nightmare.

When I was able to open my eyes against the icy blast, visibility was nil. Now I knew how Captain Oates felt as he told Scott "I am just going outside, I may be some while."

Somehow I made it despite all odds. Numbed to the bone and shaking uncontrollably from the intense cold, my trembling hands weakly pushed with all my remaining strength at the post office door. Slowly it opened and let a rush of reviving warm air into my frost bitten face. I stumbled inside accompanied by a cloud of snow and was surprised to find a queue at all counters. I surmised that these people had decided to spend the day in the post office to keep warm, save on heating costs at home and at the same time renew their cycle permit, or some other important document. I made my way to the shortest queue, which quite naturally turned out to be the slowest. But this did have the benefit that I had regained my voice and some of my composure by the time I was at the counter.

I handed over the form and my passport which were inspected closely for forgeries. They could find no fault with either and so the assistant went off in search of whatever it was that was due to me. She reappeared clutching a small envelope. As she approached I strained to see the handwriting, but all further glimpses of the letter were denied me until I had paid the fine amounting to 80 *Rappen* (38p).

I fumbled numb-fingered with my change and handed over the cash. I was rewarded with a small delicately pink tinted envelope bearing my name and address in a simple script and an insufficient British postage stamp. It did not appear to be money, but what was in this mysterious epistle? What tale did it bring to me? What news of England at Michaelmas did it bear over long and treacherous miles? I could wait no longer, so with weak and trembling hands I ripped open that little envelope right there and then.

I withdrew a colourful Christmas card depicting a traditional scene of an overloaded stage coach in the snow. All its occupants had jolly red cheeks and happy smiles on their faces, if only they knew how it really was in the snow. I opened the card and there were the immortal words that I shall take with me through the rest of my life, and beyond. Uncomplicated and yet straight to the point and delicately written in that simple hand again. It read: "Love from Chris, Jean and the girls."

I wandered back home in a daze clutching the card close to my heart in my ungloved hand. My coat was flapping open in the wind. My meagre clothing was soon stuffed with snow. I do not know how I managed to find my way back home again, but somehow I am here to tell the tale.

Anyway all that nonsense now appears to be a thing of the past thanks to the 'great ideas department' at the British Post Office who have stopped printing the price on stamps. The diligent stamp watcher at our local post office is now completely flummoxed when stamps appear before him with Her Majesty's likeness on them and bearing the legend "1st" or "2nd" where the money used to be. Great stuff!

DECEMBER 25th:

We nipped back to England for Yuletide celebrations round a good old-fashioned artificial tree with electric lights. Not to mention party hats and crackers, turkey followed by the Queen (beats Christmas Pud) and falling asleep in front of James Bond on the telly – there's nothing quite like a traditional Christmas, is there?

DECEMBER 28th:

By going to England, we missed having a white Christmas in Zurich. I have never had one, anywhere.

Back in Switzerland, after a number of winters with very little snow, there is so much snow now that it is actually hindering the skiing business. Snow has fallen on and off the whole month (but mainly on). I've found that snow does not get deeper and deeper with successive snow falls. It becomes compacted and gets harder and harder.

I had a job getting my car out of its parking space. Luckily I remembered where it was and which end was the front. There was so much snow on the car it was impossible to tell that the ski rack was on the roof. The snow plough had cleared the road and kindly sealed in the car with a hard wall of snow halfway up the doors, making them very difficult to open. Householders who had cleared their paths, had piled the snow against the back of the car to the level of the boot and to the bonnet at the front. Pushing the snow off the car only served to bury it still deeper. Fortunately, the car had been parked before the snow fell, so the road underneath was free of snow. With the car started, I had to ram it backwards and forwards in the space, bashing the snow all around into submission and then finally with a mighty roar, the car broke through the icy barricade.

It is not quite true to say that life goes on unaffected by snowfalls here. If well over a foot (32 cm) of snow fell in England, it would be a national disaster. In Zurich some buses and trams were late or cancelled. The trains got a bit out of order and a few cars drove into each other. But all in all, snow is just something else the Swiss enjoy organising. At tram stops and in the main shopping streets the snow is shovelled, quite often by mechanical diggers, into lorries and driven away. I am not quite sure where they take it, but I bet it's not wasted.

JANUARY 5th:

We went to the mountains for New Year with Regula's brother Andreas and his family. They have a holiday house in the south east corner of Switzerland. We had to take a fair bit of stuff with us, such as food and bedclothes. I had the ingenious idea of putting our duvets, pillows and ski suits into plastic bin bags, rather than using cases. Not wanting the bags to get dirty by placing them on the ground while I opened the car door, I popped them up on the car roof. With the car loaded, I then drove to the bank to get some money. An hour later, when we were ready to go, I counted the bags. Instead of three, there were only two. In a blind panic I realised that I must have left one on the roof when I drove to the bank.

That bag contained our ski suits, including an expensive new one I bought Regula for Christmas that she had not even worn yet. It was 'bin day' (or should it be bag day?) and the streets were lined with standard look-alike Swiss black plastic bags. The collection was due at any moment. I started to run back along my route to the bank. Round the corner at the end of our road I found a likely looking bag which was not as neatly placed as the others and grabbed it quickly. Passing motorists looked in alarm as I ripped it open, hoping upon hope that it was not going to be full of Frau Meier's old rubbish. To my great relief, it contained our stuff. I am now going to stop my silly habit of putting things on the roof of the car.

Regula's sister, Vroni, and family also came to the holiday house on New Year's Eve. That made a total of twelve of us there to let the New Year in. Andreas's house is in a very small village, nevertheless we managed to welcome the New Year with champagne, fireworks, and ringing church bells.

JANUARY 28th:

Assorted friends and relations from England trooped out to Switzerland during this month to try their hand (or should it be foot?) at skiing. We met up with Mark (the friend from 'van hire and friend') and wife, Maggie, at Wengen for a couple of days.

Mark's skiing may lack some polish and style, but this is more than compensated for in the plucky and fearless department. One late afternoon we were skiing back down to the village. It is a very interesting route back along paths and through fields and eventually round the houses.

We decided to stop at a restaurant at the side of the route and raced down to it. The approach was narrow and very icy. I remembered this from the previous evening and took action accordingly. Mark did not. I got there first and managed to stop and pull to one side.

This icy path ended in dry concrete with tables and chairs full of people enjoying the start of their apres ski. One side of the path was edged with a free-standing ski rack in front of a steep drop. The other side was flanked by a wooden hut with hundreds of skis and sticks neatly leaned up against it. I stopped and turned round to see where Mark was.

He was hurtling straight down the path, considerably faster than I had gone down it. His eyes told me he had seen the full horror of his situation. He had to make a quick decision. The wall of the hut with its multitude of neatly stacked skis seemed to him the least uninviting place to end this particular run.

One pair of skis can make a lot of noise when dropped. They clatter together and bounce around, so imagine the effect when about a hundred pairs and their sticks are charged at full tilt and are thrown at the sounding board of a wooden hut. The noise was like an atomic explosion. I could see what was coming and closed my eyes on impact.

Oooops!

When I opened them, the occupants of the restaurant were on their feet looking about wondering whether to run to escape the avalanche they had heard. Mark had managed somehow to go between and get behind the row of skis, taking a dozen or so of the nearest ones with him. He had gone in feet first and was lying on his side with only his head visible on the ground sticking out of an untidy pile of skis and sticks.

I had a split second to decide whether I was going to admit I was with him and face the shame, or ski on. I felt that I should stay and at least enquire if he was all right. When it became apparent that he was OK, but was unable to get out, his head started laughing in a nervously relieved sort of way. That sight was too much for me and I started laughing too and could not stop. Slowly the bemused customers of the restaurant started to sit down one by one, more amazed than amused by the antics of English tourists on skis.

Eventually we had to release his ski bindings to pull him out and the only damage was a couple of holes in his suit. The saddest thing was that not five minutes before, Mark had just used the last shot in his camera. It would have been a fantastic picture.

FEBRUARY 4th:

Regula's new job is starting to look a bit 'iffy'. Her company is an agent for buying and merging companies and does only a few deals a year. But since she joined ten months ago, they have not made a single deal.

At the end of January her boss only paid her half the money due, in cash. I was very concerned, knowing what it means when a business is down to that level and cannot pay its staff – the end is just around the corner. She was eventually paid the rest a week later. Her boss is going either senile or bust, and maybe both. She cannot get a straight answer out of him about the future, which probably says it all. It's new-job-searching-time again.

FEBRUARY 8th:

While waiting for a tram in Zurich, I noticed a man was struggling with the ticket machine. This is not unusual as all the city's bus and tram ticket machines have been replaced with computerised ones. They are highly complex and allow one to purchase a combined tram/bus/train/boat ticket to anywhere in the whole canton. The problem is that nobody has any idea how to work them.

Anyway, the man gave up and turned to me and said in a rich American accent: "The darn thing's busted. Can you work it?" I replied that it was not possible to work these new ticket machines without a degree in computer engineering. He went on fiddling with the machine and putting in coins, but still the ticket would not come out. I asked to see what he was putting in and his hand revealed an assortment of coins. Some Swiss, others German and there was even a French fifty centimes coin.

What I found so wonderful was not that he had grouped together all non-dollars into some united currency and expected them to work in a Swiss machine, but that he had turned to me and spoken in his native English and received a reply in English without batting an eyelid. Obviously he regarded this as completely normal. The tram came, he thanked me and we parted. He never expressed or showed any surprise that I was able to communicate with him. An Englishman who spoke no German, would at least start by asking the favourite British tourist opener: "Excuse me, do you speak English?" This generally elicits the favourite Swiss reply: "Of course!" That American probably went back to the USA under the impression that everybody in Switzerland speaks perfect English – which is actually not so far from the truth.

I do not mean to be rude to the Americans, if there is one nation that has mastered the art of 'perpetual tourism' then they are it. Americans seem to have the natural ability to be tourists and remain tourists, wherever they go and however long they stay away from home. This is an ability to be greatly admired, if not emulated. The American at the tram stop did not realise I was English, as another American on another tram on another day proved to me.

One evening I was travelling home after teaching. There is not much to do on a tram, so I often mark the homework that has just been handed in. A distinctively American voice asked me from behind how old the children I taught were. He had been looking over my shoulder at what I was doing.

I explained that I taught adults and we got talking about this and that. He was in his early thirties and in Zurich for some months at the University completing his post-graduate studies. After about five minutes' conversation he asked in all seriousness: "...and where did you learn your English?"

I was tempted to give a number of facetious answers, such as by watching Bugs Bunny cartoons. In the end I plumped for the rather open-ended reply: "In England."

He thought for a moment and then said quite earnestly: "Oh yeah? You know, you have a British accent!" He then said it was his stop and got off. Disappearing into the night air happily oblivious of the fact that he had complimented an Englishman on his grasp of English. Now that's a tourist.

FEBRUARY 16th:

My brother Jim and his two sons came over for a week of snow eating, alternatively known as skiing. It was their first time and they did remarkably well, which was due to their lessons on plastic in England before coming over.

The Swiss find it very funny that the British learn skiing on grassy hills covered with plastic matting. It is often a painful experience as the plastic is not as soft as snow. They felt the lessons had been a waste of time, until they got on the real stuff and found they had already learned some of the basics. Like falling and getting up again within fifteen minutes.

Things come in threes, and things falling off the roof of our car are no exception. The third rooftop loss was the skis of one of my nephews. (Firstly, Regula's watch last summer and secondly, ski suits in a bin bag in January). We had been a little careless, oh, all right, very careless about closing the ski rack on the car. We drove a number of miles slowly down to the valley from the resort after a day's skiing without any hint of what was to come. As soon as we hit the autobahn, I put my toe down. As we reached 120kph there was an ominous rattle from the roof of the car. I looked in the rear view mirror to see a pair of skis bouncing down the road behind us.

Thankfully the autobahn was very quiet and there was nobody following us when they fell off. But when the skis and the car had all come to a halt, a German in his large Mercedes happened along and ran over the skis as we watched helplessly. I trotted back down the road to recover what was left and secured the remains to the roof. The skis had seen some good wear before we hired them, but now they were minus the bindings which had been crushed and broken off beneath the wheels of the Mercedes.

The next morning my brother went back apologetically to the hire shop clutching the remaining pieces. The man in the ski hire shop was unconcerned and he tossed the bits in a bin of similarly smashed skis. It seems that this sort of thing happens about once a week and he was well insured. However the man noticed the bindings were gone and asked where they were. My young nephew was able to put him clearly in the picture and advised him that the bindings were, as he put it, "smashed to smiv-ver-weens."

FEBRUARY 26th:

"Thump!" That is the sound of the Swiss tax form landing in the letter box again. This time we managed to fill it in without the help of Regula's father. He just checked it when we had finished. We had made a trip to the tax office a few weeks ago, because we were not happy with the final assessment of last year's tax return. We had been very honest and declared that we still have a house in England, so they charged us tax on it thank you very much. (No sooner had we shaken off the poll tax than we fell straight into this trap.) The amount involved was about Sfr 400, enough to send us to sort things out with the tax man, who far from being a pompous little Hitler in a pinstripe suit, turned out to be a pompous aging hippy in a hand-knitted sweater.

He took pity on our plight and said we could halve the value we had put down for the house. I think that was for our trouble in going there. I mentioned that I had a mortgage on the property and said that surely should be set against tax too. To our surprise he agreed to this. This year we are optimistic (and why not) that we can cut our tax bill.

MARCH 15th:

March is notable for us in that it contains both our birthdays. On the subject of feeling one's age, which of course I do not, I had an aging experience on a ski holiday earlier in the month.

One evening at dinner we sat next to a ski instructor who came from Montreal. I brightly informed him that I had visited the World's Fair there. He was somewhat puzzled as he had never heard of it and he asked when it took place. I told him it was the summer of 1968. Through a faint smile he nodded and replied, "That was two years before I was born." He was a bit of a plonker anyway.

March can bring a very strange mixture of weather. The mountains are still snow covered and the ski season is going hell-for-leather, but in the lowlands spring is already creeping in. These first mild breezes lead us to consider a cycling holiday in the summer. To train we decided to repeat my last year's solo achievement of reaching Germany by bike. With passports and sandwiches carefully packed, we set off. The winter months had taken their toll and unfortunately we could only reach the halfway mark before having to turn back.

On our return we discovered that Regula's physique had suffered in a number of places, but mainly where it came into contact with the bicycle. Thus a new saddle and handle bars are on her birthday present list and we are now considering a walking holiday instead.

MARCH 26th:

We have bought a video recorder. The old one which was that famous Scottish brand Akai (ach aye), works fine in the UK, but will only play in Switzerland (a bit like me really) and not record due to the different trans-mission frequencies. Technology has marched relentlessly on since we bought the last video. We found what we wanted and it even has a VPS button. This stands for 'very popular switch', which is not surprising when you learn that it changes the on and off times of preprogrammed recordings when they are transmitted behind schedule. We have twenty-five TV channels and it took the best part of a whole evening to program them into the video recorder. I made the error of unplugging it overnight and spent the next day reprogramming it. This was not as easy as it said in the instructions, which of course were in the four Swiss languages – German, French, Japanese and English.

MARCH 23rd:

Regula's job staggers on, with no sign of business improving. They seem to realise that if they do not pay her she will leave. They do not want to lose her, so they are doubly nice to her. We hope they will also pay her at the end of this month.

The good people of the Canton of Zurich went to the polls. This time it was for a real election – that is for people, not a proposition. It is a confusing picture to say the least, particularly when you are used to the unfair, but understandable two-party British system. In the Canton there was a choice of no less than twenty-three parties and the result was bewildering to an English tourist.

Regula was not too much help explaining it either. She spent hours, as usual, pouring over the papers beforehand only to arrive at the polling station minutes before it closed. She is not really sure if those she voted for got in or not. But then she cannot remember all the people she voted for anyway. This is not quite as daft as it sounds, if you had seen the ballot papers, you would be confused too. On some sheets you even have the possibility to write in the candidates' names yourself. What happens if you mis-spell their names? Or Willy Müller is confused with Billy Müller?

APRIL 2nd:

London saw its last tram in 1952 (a double-decker of course). For the British, trams represent an old-fashioned noisy and slow mode of transport. English visitors are surprised and impressed by Zurich's modern tram system. The more so when they learn it runs to a strict timetable.

Connoisseurs of London Transport, who are used to buses travelling in convoys of three every half hour, do not believe that a timetable is possible in crowded city traffic. But if a Zurich tram is a minute or so late, waiting passengers become uneasy and start to inspect the timetable at the tram stop and look at their watches. When the tram arrives the driver is given black looks and expected to explain his waywardness. Tram drivers seem in a constant frenzy to keep to the timetable, they will actually leave passengers behind who are obviously dashing to catch the tram.

APRIL 13th:

The 'begging' letters continue to arrive by nearly every post. I estimate that at least half our mail is a request for money for some cause or other. How many of these are genuine is anybody's guess. We are now sending all such letters back unopened and marked '*refusé*' in the hope that they will stop. The number of people on the street soliciting cash is growing too, often this is for no higher ideal than to service a hangover.

New blue-zone parking regulations are around the corner and that is where they can stay. The next thing Zurich's red/green council have put their minds to is the rubbish. We have been informed how much extra we will have to pay for the privilege of having our plastic bags taken away. It is calculated on the number of rooms one's flat or house has. The more rooms you have the more you pay. We will have to pay Sfr 173 for what was essentially free before, although it was actually included in the taxes, and still will be. This extra charge is to be levied to finance a new rubbish-treatment plant.

However this is only the thin edge of the wedge – phase two involves the rubbish being permitted only in 'official' bags. So if you leave your rubbish out in any old bag they will not take it away. The catch is that these official bags will be expensive (somewhere between 1 and 5 francs each, depending on size).

The idea is to stop people putting out so much rubbish. This may sound daft, because you cannot expect people to keep their rubbish, but it is to stop manufacturers and shops from wrapping and packing their wares so much. Supermarkets have to provide bins for shoppers to throw away the excess packaging. It seems at times that 50% of what we bring home is packaging, so this could be a good move, but it is an odd way to go about it. When I worked for a brief period in the toy trade it was said of the toy manufacturers that they sold you the box and gave you the contents free. It seems to me that it should be the manufacturers who are penalised, not the customers.

This new rubbish regime will add more stress to the life of the already stressed Swiss citizen. It will make people fill their rubbish bags to bursting, or leave their rubbish outside other peoples' houses. There is already a phenomenon known as 'rubbish tourism' in areas that already operate this system. This means that people take their rubbish 'on holiday' in ordinary bags to another community that does not require rubbish to be left in expensive official bags. No doubt there will be a squad of highly trained 'rubbish police' to enforce these new rules.

All in a day's work for the Zurich rubbish police.

Swiss rubbish has long been sorted into various categories like glass, paper and aluminium for recycling purposes. When my wife first lived in England, she made me phone our local council to ask where she could dispose of her old cooking oil. The environment department at the council had no system for dealing with used oil and no plans for doing anything about it in the future. The Brits, shock and horror, tip their chip-pan oil down the drain.

The Swiss love of the English language finds its way into every walk of life. Paper that is reused is called 'recycling paper'. I point out to my students when we reach the passive tenses, that this should be 'recycled paper'. Like the favourite drink of Swiss school children, 'ice tea', which should be 'iced tea'. (What a thing to do to tea.) It is only a matter of time before someone asks me why we say 'ice cream' and not 'iced cream'. The answer is that 'ice cream' is not the same as 'iced cream'. However that still leaves me wondering why, when shops are not 'closed', they are 'open', not 'opened'.

APRIL 15th:

We go to the cinema more than we did in England. The reason is threefold. Firstly living in a cramped flat with no garden means we need to get out more. Secondly the films shown in Zurich are in their original language, thus usually English or mumbling American. Thirdly the choice available is extensive and there has been a crop of good, or reasonably good films released in the last few years. We saw the saddest film of the decade, *Awakenings*, about patients who came out of comas after twenty-five years only to go barmy. It left me depressed and in a state of shock for the following twenty-four hours, but otherwise undamaged. We tend to go for the light and easy escape film in the genre of 'When Harry met the Pretty Woman at the Dead Poets' Society for a Green Card at my Table' not to mention 'Dances with Oscars'.

APRIL 20th:

I bought a video camera to record things for posterity. But, as it seems with everything I buy these days, the video camera was not a simple purchase. I knew that Super 8 was out, as we have a VHS system like everyone else. (If you were suckered into buying Beta-max, I suggest you keep quiet about it.)

The Japanese like to write daft things all over their video cameras, but it has not stopped people buying them. The more you pay, the more outlandish are the things printed on the camera. What with 'Autofocus' '8x Zoom' 'CCD' 'Stereo' '400 Pixels' 'Long Play' and so on, there is hardly any blank space on

FINGER TIP VIDEO BATTERY PACK

FINGER TIP V.D.

MORE THINGS THAN WILL FIT HERE

MUCH BETTER THAN YOURS MK III

The camera cannot lie, just exaggerate a bit.

the cameras. The daftest one I saw was 'State of the Art'. I hope that could be peeled off when it was not any more. What they are really trying to say is "Better Than Yours" "Top of The Range" "I'm a Professional at This" and "I'm Jones, can you keep up with me?" or even "Beat that, Sucker!"

Our local EPA store (pronounced: eh-pa, a sort of clean Swiss Woolies) has just opened a new restaurant and boasts that its men's toilet has a table for changing babies' nappies. Where will it all end? Perhaps I will nip up there with the video camera...

MAY 2nd:

A student at Look & Learn was very surprised and pleased to find his bicycle, that had been stolen about a week before, chained to a lamp post outside the building where the school is. He phoned the police, who advised that they were nearly all taking the day off after shooting rubber bullets at May Day demonstrators, but recommended that he cut the chain and bring the bike to them to record the details. He could then keep the bike if he was sure it was his.

However enquiries within the school revealed that a young man doing another course had made his way there on that self-same machine. That student advised that he had exchanged it for a moped with a friend of his. Unfortunately, he was unable to recall the name of his friend and seemed very relieved to learn that the police were unable to come. Student A went home happy on his recovered bike and student B went off trying to remember the name of his friend. My only question was "has student B paid for his course?" The answer to which was "his friend paid."

MAY 4th:

The UK tax man has still not decided anything about my status. They must think that I am up to something (I wish I were). The Swiss tax man has so far accepted our tax return. We have to wait until the end of the year to know if it has passed the fine-tooth-comb-check. If our Swiss tax return is accepted we will have cut our tax bill since last year. Stepping through the tax jungle is quite an art here. I have found out that one can deduct a fee for preparing (in other words filling in) the tax form itself. So next time around I can cut our tax still further.

How do taxes compare? Well I wish I could tell you about millionaires, they are apparently well catered for in Switzerland. But even us ordinary folk are better off than in Britain. Our combined incomes are about the same as they were in the UK. There we paid 32% of our incomes in tax and National Health contributions. In Switzerland this figure, including our private health insurance fund, is under 20%.

MAY 7th:

We went to the second wedding of a former work colleague of Regula. The couple met in therapy, so when her ten-year-old son was asked who the shabbily-dressed, noisy stranger was at the reception, he replied in all innocence "Oh, that's my mummy's psychiatrist."

MAY 11th:

We now both have matching black 'his' and 'hers' cycle shorts, with extra padding bits where the saddle goes. This is only a stage in a long series of 'carrots' to try and get Regula out on her bike again. I have already swopped her handlebars round so that they turn upwards and she does not have to bend down so much. Then I bought a new saddle for her – a British Brooks leather one no less, the best that money can buy. But that was too hard and she eyed my bike's saddle. So I swopped them over, the saddle from my bike is softer, but alas not big enough. So the cycle trousers were the next step, but finally perhaps only an armchair will suffice.

MAY 30th:

After probably the worst May in living memory weather-wise, summer suddenly arrived. We are puzzled as to what happened to spring, as we have gone directly from winter into summer. But it arrived and that is what is important. The tables and chairs of cafés and restaurants are out in the streets again. The bathing areas along the lake have re-opened, but the water is still too nippy for me.

JUNE 1st:

Back to the theme of Swiss rubbish; we thought only private house-holders were paying more for rubbish collections. The new surcharge (added to our electric bill, by the way) works out at Sfr 2.50 for every bag we put out. The Look & Learn school have a small container that is normally emptied twice a week. They will now have to pay Sfr 35 for each collection. How do the powers-that-be check that? Each container is fitted with a small sealed meter that clocks on each time the container is tipped upside down into the back of the dust cart. So what can the school do to cut down on this new expense? Padlocks appear to be the answer. One to keep the lid closed and stop other people putting their rubbish into it and another to chain it to the building to stop it being inadvertently inverted.

JUNE 3rd:

In an effort to reduce 'summer smog' the speed limit on certain stretches of the Swiss autobahns is to be reduced to 100kph (60mph) for private cars and 70kph (42mph) for lorries and cars towing caravans. This will just apply to the months of July and August when the roads are usually so full of holiday traffic and road works that it is impossible to drive any faster anyway. Quite how they will enforce the limits is unclear. Automatic radar is feasible, but it cannot distinguish between a car and a lorry.

There was a big song and dance about the speed limits, from both the policy's proponents and the increasing lobby against the continued bashing of the car. The papers print the daily smog levels and the TV news announces them before the weather forecast.

Summer smog does not seem all that much to worry about to me. I have never noticed it or any of its supposed effects. Secondly experts cannot even agree on whether slowing down the traffic will make matters better or worse. There is a theory that suggests that vehicles will run less efficiently at these lower speeds and emit higher levels of pollutants.

Unlike speed limits in the UK, which are spread by word of mouth, and where 60 and 70mph speed limits are still indicated by the pre-1966 derestricted sign of a black slash on a white background, the Swiss speed limits will be dealt with in true Swiss fashion. This means new signs will be installed on all the sections of autobahns concerned.

These will then be removed again after two months. I thought the government was short of money.

However if the Swiss government are really interested in the public's health, they would be far better advised to spend their time and money on stopping people smoking. 2.5 million Swiss, or about half the adult population, smoke. There is a law which stipulates that Zurich restaurants must provide a no-smoking area. But this is not enforced and in many restaurants my meals are ruined by other people's smoke drifting across my food. Surely smoking is much more annoying, not to say lethal, than any passing summer smog? But then, I'm just a tourist.

Swash tray

JUNE 5th:

Zurich town council continues to get a lousy press and the latest is they have run out of money, having spent a lot on various social schemes. A familiar tale and so is the remedy. We are to pay more tax to help them out and cuts in services are on the way. In the meantime businesses, which are already hard pushed with Zurich traffic and the general problems of a big city, are moving out. Their departure results in even less tax revenue for the city. Lack of cash has not stopped the digging up of the roads and renovating of buildings everywhere.

The road at the bottom of ours has been dug up along its length for the last six months as 'far heating' is installed. This means that instead of having everyone with their own polluting oil-fired boiler, there is just one big polluting boiler that heats the buildings for the whole community. This new heating system is expensive and few seem to want it (and of course the road needs to be dug up, I am not quite sure why for six months though).

Next in line for the 'far heating' treatment is our road. I do not know where we will park the car for six months – probably in the other road, if it has been put back together by then, as they parked in ours while theirs was dug up. The Müllers (our landlords) have been told by the 'fire police' that they must replace their oil-fired boiler as its fumes do not meet the city's pollution standards. It is much cheaper for them to replace their boiler than have the 'far heating' brought near.

The theory of 'far heating' (I am sure it must be called something else in English, like 'very-central heating') is a good one. The heat is produced by burning rubbish in incinerators. We buy goods with packing on, for which the manufacturers charge us. We then throw the packing away and the council charge us handsomely for collecting it. They then burn it and heat water with it and charge us for the hot water.

JUNE 14th:

I wrote some while ago about the exotic places the 'ordinary' Swiss go to for their holidays. I have a new student at Look & Learn who is a postman and is going to Indonesia for a holiday of four months. I asked him why Indonesia and he explained that he had been to most of the other places like Hong Kong, Australia and America and he had always fancied Indonesia. He even complains that the postmen are not very well paid. I daren't tell him they speak Dutch and not English in Indonesia.

Then there was the man on the till in the *Bahnhof Buffet* (railway station self-service restaurant) where I go once a week for lunch with other English teachers from St Addanuf. He had been away for a couple of weeks and returned looking tanned. He had been in the Caribbean, Santa Lucia to be precise. He further surprised his audience of agog English teachers by adding that it was not a very expensive holiday at all.

JUNE 25th:

Amongst items voted on by the good people of Zurich was a proposal to ban fruit-machine arcades in the Canton. (Fruit machines were once called 'one armed bandits', but the march of technology has made them armless.) They are already banned in most other cantons. Payouts are higher at Sfr 100 than the pub-type ones in the UK and it is felt that far too many people are giving far too much money to these machines. The proposal was accepted. Low jackpots and video games are still allowed, but they do not earn the big money that the fruit machines do and so it should be impossible for most arcades to continue. The result of the proposal is being vigorously fought against by the owners of the arcades, who are taking the matter to court.

JUNE 28th:

We returned from a shopping expedition at our local Coop supermarket loaded with bags as usual. When we unpacked we were unable to find a number of things we thought we had bought. We concluded that we (or rather I) must have left one of the bags of assorted foodstuffs in the supermarket after paying for it at the checkout.

Next morning Regula phoned them up and sure enough they had it. We went to collect our missing bag, wondering what state our cream, yoghurt and cheese would be in after a night in the warm. We were very impressed to find that they had returned these items to the cool cabinets and asked if we would select fresh ones. Good old Coop! We'll leave our stuff there again.

JULY 1st:

It's July and the authorities are not ready to enforce the new 100/70kph speed limits. New speed-limit signs will not all be in place until the third week of the month. They will no sooner have them up and it will be time to take them down again.

Zurich's red/green council did not want to be left out of the car bashing act. They decided to ban all motorised traffic from the central area of town for the months of July and August. This met with howls of protest from shop owners and some incredulity from the public, who were under the impression that such measures required at least some sort of vote from them. However, as the council only thought it up one quiet Friday afternoon a week ago, they had to abandon the idea.

JULY 8th:

We spent a very pleasant, if very wet Sunday in the Bern area for the confirmation of one of Regula's many godchildren. As always in Switzerland this involved lots of eating and in the Bern area they are particularly famous for this.

Eighteen of us, family and friends, went to a local restaurant where a private room had been hired. We sat down at 12.30 to an excellent lunch. We eventually left at a quarter to five, having eaten nearly continuously, then proceeded to the family's home for, you guessed it, more eating and drinking.

On a rainy day, when you cannot do much else, eating out is not a bad idea. This long distance eating is much more common than in England where getting your food down as quickly as possible to do something more important is the order of the day. The British regard meal times as an intrusion into the business of the day, whereas the Swiss often regard meal times as the business of the day. That is of course mainly at weekends and public holidays. However, even on workdays the Swiss often have a longer lunch break than the British. In Switzerland lunch is the main meal of the day with only a little to eat in the evening. At weekends in the country, restaurants are full of people who sit for hours talking, eating and drinking and often playing cards.

There are no pubs in Switzerland, as there are in Britain, where one can only buy beer and a bag of crisps. In Switzerland you can just drink in a restaurant if you like or you can have a snack or a full-blown meal. You will be asked when you come in if you want to eat, which always seems like a daft question to ask someone entering a restaurant.

JULY 10th:

Sorry to harp on about the weather again, but it will not take long. Switzerland lies on the dividing line between northern and southern European weather. This means we get about four days of Mediterranean weather with temperatures up to 28°C followed by four days of northern weather of 14°C. The quick changes are accompanied by big thunderstorms and can be confusing for the man in the street.

You can observe people who missed the weather forecast, or simply did not look through their triple glazing at their thermometers before they went out. They are easily spotted on hot days, sweating in the tram under their overcoats, or conversely in their shirt sleeves at tram stops hopping from one foot to the other to keep warm on cold days.

JULY 20th:

Zurich cinemas really push their wares at a bi-annual *Kino Spektakel* (Cinema Spectacular) when about 200 films are shown throughout the town 24 hours a day for three days non-stop at special low admission prices. We planned to see lots of films we missed when they were first shown, but we ended up seeing only the late night showing of *Indiana Jones and the Last Crusade*. This includes Sean Connery with his usual supply of suitable words with S's in.

("Mr Shpielberg thish shcrip sheems to be shimply shplattered with shuperfluoush and shpurioush S'sh.") Buses ran specially through the night so that cinema goers could get home – shplendid.

(This paragraph is for Beatles fans.) I see that in a sort of 'Ebony and Irony' Paul McCartney has written a piece of classical music. Could this be 'Mary had a Little Symphony'? Or why not 'Sergeant Pepper's Lonely Hearts Club Orchestra'? It is all enough to make John Lennon roll over in his Beethoven. Other classical McCartney pieces might include 'A Hard Day's Nachtmusik' – 'I want to hold your Handel' – 'You've gotta Hayden your Love away' – 'Bach in the USSR', 'Albinoni the Lonely' (oh sorry that was Roy Orbison's). Perhaps Paul McCartney should change his name to Johan Scouse?

The UK tax man wrote and agreed at last that I am resident abroad. Then reassessed my tax for the year before I left the UK and paid me back £200, which I did not think I was entitled to. But don't worry. It is not possible to win with the tax authorities. They are now working on the next year and I reckon they will want it back, and more.

JULY 28th:

They did! You know the tax people – from a week ago. They had no sooner sent me a £200 refund for one year to butter me up than they sent a demand for £500 tax due for the following year.

AUGUST 3rd – 17th:

With surfboard on the car, it is back to England for a couple of weeks in the wind and a visit to the dentist.

Whilst over in Britain I noted a new preoccupation amongst its inhabitants. When friends meet, the conversation leads quickly to the subject of one's cholesterol level. When I blithely declared that I had no idea what my cholesterol level was, I was greeted with gasps of disbelief. Surely I must have had it checked? I had not. I tried to counter with one or two of the obsessions near to the Swiss heart; such as enquiring what the ozone level was, or where the nearest aluminium-recycling collection point was. This only met with blank gazes and further strong demands that I should not be so careless with my body and should have my cholesterol level checked at once.

I noticed on the French autoroute where I stopped for lunch on the way back from England that a quarter litre of soft drink costs ten Frenchy francs. This is the same price as an equal quantity of local red wine. And they wonder why their accident rate is so high.

The car's silencer was less silent when I got back to Switzerland. It cost Sfr 250 to replace. I should have had it done in England, it would have been cheaper. There are not many places that fit new silencers while you wait in Switzerland. This is because most Swiss people sell their car long before the silencer needs replacing.

AUGUST 20th:

With a new silencer on the car I went to my brother-in-law and doctor, Andreas, to have my cholesterol level measured along with my blood pressure. How the Swiss like gadgets! Doc A has a machine that measures blood functions – pressure and pulse. He had picked it up at a scrap yard. Another doctor had thrown it out as it was over twelve months old. Andreas reckons anything that impresses the patients is worth another 15% on his bill. I tried not to be too impressed. His nurse fixed the band to my arm and left me alone to contemplate the cut on my finger she had just made to check my cholesterol. Then every two minutes the little computer-like machine pumped up the arm band and took my blood pressure and pulse and then printed both values out with the date and time. However, the time was two minutes and thirty seconds slow. I pointed this out to Andreas and asked if the other figures could be relied upon. He said they could and they were a little bit on the high side. A little alteration to the psychological diet and I shall be back in a few months to see if the figures are lower. I wish I had not bothered, I preferred to live in ignorance.

AUGUST 28th – SEPTEMBER 2nd:

A couple of English pals with the unlikely names of Chris and Chris are forever being caught up in complicated holiday arrangements. They are man and wife (Christopher and Christine). With Swiss logic Regula devised the idea of calling them "Chris the man" and "Chris the woman." We meet up with them whenever they venture in our general direction. This time they got themselves involved in some timeshare apartment in Austria and we arranged to visit them for a long weekend.

We left Zurich on the Budapest overnight express on Thursday evening. I made the reservations and managed to make a pig's ear of them. I forgot to be a tourist and made the reservations in German. We were leaving at 23.45 on the 28th, but all of the journey, bar the first fifteen minutes, was on the 29th, I somehow thought in my fuzzy German that I should be booking for the 29th, particularly since we needed separate tickets for Austria and they were for the 29th. The train tickets were valid, but the reservations for the couchettes were for the 29th, the following night. We had to try and find two seats in a train packed with excited Hungarians homeward bound with pockets full of hard-earned Swiss francs.

The only seats we could find were in a first class compartment with four people from Hong Kong. They were looking for somewhere to settle before the Chinese take-over and the railway compartment seemed ideal.

We spent the rest of the night being disturbed by ticket inspectors, passport checkers and other passengers desperately searching for somewhere to sit. We arrived at our destination bleary eyed at 7.30 am. It was our first time in Austria and we were favourably impressed. Houses and villages are at times almost too pretty and cute and covered with too many flowers. The food was excellent with whipped cream over everything they could think of. Prices were lower than Switzerland, which is not too difficult an achievement.

Our return-journey couchette reservations were fine, but the couchettes themselves were too hard for much sleep. It did really maximise our time, giving us three full days away.

Poor Regula just had time to nip to our flat from the station on Monday morning for a shower and change, then she was straight off to the office for 9 o'clock. Not that I could catch up on missed sleep. Our peace is being completely shattered for the next few months while a trench some three metres (12ft) deep is being dug right down our road to install 'far heating'. The only person who wants it, lives in the last house in the road.

SEPTEMBER 6th:

We were swimming at a local lake and kept hearing a budgie chirping away. I scoured the skies, the trees and the grass, but could not see one. Eventually I pinpointed the source of the chirping. It was coming from the direction of an old couple who appeared blissfully unaware of it.

I went over to see what it was. There on the ground between their sunloungers was their pet budgie in its cage, chatting away to itself in its little mirror. After that I was on the lookout for goldfish being taken for a swim in the lake.

SEPTEMBER 10th:

That odd Monday afternoon Zurich holiday came round again – 'Boys Shooting'. Now with 25% of contestants girls for the first time, the name doesn't fit so well. Letting girls in was part of the loony left's less loony ideas. But here is a good one for you and an idea that has been seriously aired recently in Switzerland: an official meter installed in every private car to record the distance driven each year! People who drove more than 8000 kms per year would pay for each extra kilometre. But, and this is the best bit, drivers who drove less than 8000 kms would be paid an 'ecology bonus' for saving energy. Can you imagine trying to administer this?

It is an infringement of personal freedom making the private car no longer private. First it was 'the spy in the cab' for lorries, now it could be 'the spy in the car'. Wait for 'the spy in the loo' to check the water usage. If the government want people to drive less, then they should make petrol more expensive. Swiss petrol is currently the cheapest in Europe. But not for long. There is a plan to raise petrol prices by 20%. I know what will happen. We will end up having both meters and dearer petrol. Time to think like a tourist again.

SEPTEMBER 13th:

In a land heavy with laws and preoccupied with their enforcement, Zurich folk were surprised that the police were unable to find a law to prevent a man from painting his own parking space with yellow paint on a city street outside his office. I would very much like to paint my own space in the road outside our flats, but there is a hole three metres deep where my parking space used to be.

OCTOBER 4th:

I already feel like an old professional at teaching. My sister-in-law in England, who recently started teaching children with learning disabilities, wrote asking what tips I could give her. My number one rule is: don't teach children. Rule number two is: only teach people who want to be taught and have paid to be taught. Sadly she had broken the first two rules straight off. Still she may have better luck with my third rule: never cry in front of your class.

A survey in one of my 'teach yourself to teach' books reveals that students say the most important attribute a teacher should have is the ability to make classes interesting.

Easy to say, but hard to do. At the end of this term a student was leaving and she said that she would like to make a small announcement. She stood up and said that she had enjoyed the class and went on to say in her commendable, but still rather weak English "I hope that Mr Bilton will give you more interesting lessons next term." And I thought they were already interesting.

OCTOBER 5th – 12th:

The autumn break found us back in Ticino. We slipped out of Zurich and headed south on a dull and cool Friday morning. We lunched at a hotel at the south end of the spectacular Urnersee at the foot of the valley which climbs up to the St Gotthard tunnel and pass.

Swiss specialities change with the seasons and autumn brings *wild menüs*. Not quite as exciting as it may first sound; in English these are game dishes. The game was venison and we played. We drank *Sauser*, this year's partly fermented wine, which is red, a little bubbly, low in alcohol and is good for diarrhoea (getting it, not stopping it). Also available at this time of year is vermicelli, chestnut puree with cream and meringue for sweet.

While we ate, the windsurfers' dream, the *Föhn*, started with a vengeance. It blew around leaves, plastic bags and the occasional tourist. This did not bode well for us as it meant lousy weather south of the Alps. Outside after lunch the temperature had gone up by 8°C. In the excitement I left my sunglasses on the dining table. We then put the car to the ultimate test and instead of the eighteen-kilometre long tunnel, we drove over the St Gotthard Pass to a height of 2100 metres (6400ft).

Since a Bournemouth supermarket car-park in August, the car had suffered on and off with a leaking radiator. I was now onto my forth bottle of HOLT'S RADWELD, a remarkable product which is a disgusting sludge that, when poured in a car's leaking radiator, seals holes. It first saved my bacon over twenty years ago. There were four of us going on a camping holiday to Spain. My friend, whose car we were travelling in, had joined the AA (Automobile Association, not Alcoholics Anonymous) to take advantage of their Five Star Continental touring insurance. We packed the car to bursting and filled the roof-rack with tents and camping equipment and set off for the evening ferry to France.

When we had gone no more than two miles, the radiator boiled over. We opened the bonnet and the problem was clear. That afternoon my friend had fixed his new AA badge to the front grill. The screws supplied were long and in his enthusiasm he had merrily screwed one of them into the radiator. How many AA patrolmen can have been called out to a breakdown caused by their own badges? That was my first introduction to RADWELD. It got us to Spain and back without a problem. So we considered that the Gotthard Pass would put our RADWELD-filled radiator to the ultimate test.

Before the trip I had been to a scrap yard to look for a second-hand radiator. Yes, there are scrap yards in Switzerland and they are in many ways a miniature version of the country itself. Entry is restricted, but the main gate welcomes those who come to spend money. Once inside, the scrap yard is carefully arranged into row after row of neat heaps of cars on top of each other, making the best use of the limited space available. Prices are high, but these are not just any scrapped cars, they are Swiss scrapped cars. All neat and efficient. But not that efficient; they did not have a radiator to fit my car.

We reached the top of the Gotthard Pass without difficulty and stayed overnight at the old hospice where the stage coaches once stopped. It is a forlorn place today, well off the beaten track ever since the tunnel was opened in 1980. The creaky old bedrooms have hand-painted ceilings and china washing bowls, jugs and chamber pots. Were it not for the Swiss army, who play lots of games nearby (sharpening their knives, etc.), the place would be deserted.

As predicted the weather got worse. Visibility was only twenty-five metres in the swirling fog of wet clouds and it rained continuously. The next day we descended to Ticino, where the rain was to continue for the next four days. We had booked an apartment blindly and it turned out to be very nice. We found out, when the mists eventually cleared, that it had fine views over the Lago di Lugano (that's the lake). It was 400 metres (1200ft) above Lugano in the little artists' village of Carona.

The apartment was modern, warm and well equipped. It even had satellite TV including British Sky News and Sky One, which we do not get in Zurich. If you are thinking of a satellite dish, then my advice is: save your money. It is 'lowest common denominator TV'. They show what gets the biggest audiences and thus pulls in the most advertisers. The result is a twenty-four-hours-a-day diet of American wrestling, sensational Australian documentaries and 'Blind Date'. Okay, so I was wrong and it sounds like just what you always wanted.

During four days of rain, other than putting our marriage to the test, we made a number of umbrella excursions to Lugano. During one of these trips a multi-storey car park managed to do what neither the St Gotthard Pass nor the trip back from England could. It got the radiator to boil over.

We managed to chug slowly out of town in the car but soon had to pull up on a garage forecourt in a cloud of steaming RADWELD. It was the forecourt of an Opel dealer, who for Sfr 480 said they would fit a new radiator. We had no choice. The next day the weather was brighter and we set out by boat on the start of a long walk skilfully devised to end at the premises of the Opel dealer to collect the repaired car.

After an all too brief bright spell, the holiday ended in more disgusting weather which had been prepared some twenty-four hours earlier in Britain. There is no use in denying it, we could see it on satellite TV. Idiots at Blackpool in PAKAMACs walking at forty-five degrees along the front as thirty foot waves broke over them and a Pickfords van lying its side on the M6 motorway.

The fact that it rained solidly for 60% of our holiday, that the car had needed expensive repairs and that the video camera had gone on the blink (still under guarantee) all paled into insignificance compared to the homeward journey. We set out late on Saturday afternoon full to the gunnels with holiday stuff and Regula's parents who visited us for the last two days. After half an hour up the autobahn towards the Gotthard tunnel, the engine started misfiring and lost power. At the next exit, we left the autobahn and bumped, rattled and exploded our way into some unheard of Italian-speaking village at 5.30 on a wet Saturday evening.

We came to rest on the forecourt of a filling station and made our problem known to the understanding proprietors. They shook their heads knowingly when they heard the engine. I guessed it was big ends – *grosse endi*. But was proved wrong. The mechanical consensus was *ventili*, a valve. A valve that was not doing whatever it is valves should.

This was helping my knowledge of car parts in Italian, but it meant 'big bucks' in any language. They confirmed that the car was still driveable in an up-and-down-the-road sort of way. On the question of the 200 km run to Zurich and the Gotthard tunnel, they were less enthusiastic. Repairs could only be started in a week at the earliest and would cost more than the value of the car. The nice young man whose father owned the garage offered to 'black taxi' us and our luggage back to Zurich for "only" Sfr 300. I removed the number plates and the radio and we left our car there. We agreed the garage owner would phone to tell us the scrap value. It had a good radiator and a relatively new exhaust. On our journey back we stopped at that same hotel again by the Urnersee and I was able to recover my sunglasses, so all was not lost.

OCTOBER 26th:

We got back to Zurich in time for yet another vote. This time it was the five-yearly national government elections. Talk about democracy gone mad! The Swiss voting papers are delivered to voters' homes four weeks before the election. This is for the best, as it would take all day to fill in the ballot papers at the polling booth. There are 246 seats in the Swiss national parliament, divided amongst thirteen different parties. With no clear majority, the government is always a coalition.

There is a wide choice of parties. These range from the conventional to the Swiss equivalent of the Monster Raving Loony Party, such as the 'Thank Goodness we've got Beat Loser' party. Beat Loser is a young man who goes to the same tailor as Robin Hood, if his campaign posters are anything to go by. The 'Laws Against Disadvantaged Men' party is a sort of Men's Lib party. A green party for the elderly called the 'Naturally Over 60', known as the Swiss Greys. There is a sinister sounding 'National Action Party Against Over-foreigning', if they get in I could be on my way back to England (but I bet even they love tourists). There is even a Car Party, which won two seats at the last election, no doubt they were bucket seats. They are for the downtrodden lot of the car and driver, and are a reaction to the hammering that the motorist has to take from the Green lobby.

In the Canton of Zurich there are thirty-four official parties on the ballot sheet for voters to muse over. I say official, because a blank ballot sheet is also supplied, so that voters can make up their own ideal party out of candidates from any combination of the other parties. Voters can delete a name and enter their own candidate on the ballot sheet, as long as they are Swiss and over eighteen. (You'll find their date of birth in their ski-trousers). I expected the results of these elections about four months after the polls closed. They came within hours.

The issues for debate in Switzerland are quite different to those in Britain where such subjects as the economy, National Health Service, unemployment, inflation and education are hot topics. The Swiss have a whole different set of issues to think about. The environment, traffic, the drug problem, political asylum seekers, personal freedom and the European Union are the things that the Swiss worry and wring their hands about.

OCTOBER 29th:

The news on our car is not good. A colleague who works at Look & Learn and comes from Ticino phoned the garage there for me. This involved a lot of shouting and gesticulating in Italian over the phone.

The garage owner said the car was worthless and he charged Sfr 25 to drive cars to the scrap yard. After a bit more long-distance shouting and arm waving the garage owner agreed to drive it there for nothing. When asked about the new radiator fitted not two days before the breakdown, he advised that we have been diddled and that it is not new. One thing is true the world over – you can never win with cars, they will always cost you money one way or another.

On the subject of cars, my two nephews were interested to learn that Manta jokes were all the rage here for a couple of weeks, which is longer than the car itself was popular. A 'Manta' being a sports car named after a flat fish. It has a better ring to it than the Opel 'Dab' or even 'Flounder'. I have to say the jokes are not all that funny, like – "they are now making Mantas only two-feet wide so that the drivers can rest their elbows on both doors." "What causes the red stripe a metre high on the garage wall?" Answer: "Manta drivers." (Their elbows do it.(Ooh!)) I prefer the old Skoda jokes like – a man went into a garage and said "Any chance of a wing mirror for a Skoda?" The garage man replied "Yeah, sounds like a fair swop to me!"

NOVEMBER 1st:

Regula put an ad in the paper under a box number in her attempt to look for a new job and received twenty-five replies. Unfortunately half were from job agencies, and the other half from companies out of the way or offering jobs that had nothing to do with what she wanted. Her ad was a waste, but she spotted in the same paper what appears to be an ideal job. She phoned them up and went for an interview. The job is with a large insurance company, working 80% with Fridays off. Most of the work is in English, the people are nice and the pay is as good as her present job, but with much more security. What's even better, she got the job.

NOVEMBER 6th:

We have another car! We had a rough idea what we wanted in a car: a good radiator and sturdy valves being high on the list. We saw an Audi 80 CD (which no doubt stands for 'conned diabolically') for sale privately in the paper. After a bit of test driving and haggling it was ours. Dull grey, four dull doors, we are dull but mobile again.

At the road traffic office we have managed to get lower numbered plates than before. The first number could have stayed with me for life, but I gave the old plates back for credit for the weeks we were off the road. The new plates may have a lower number, but they are shiny and new. The sooner they look shabby and have a few holes drilled through them, the more fashionable they will be. In Britain it is the opposite, where owners of old cars try to brighten them up with new number-plates.

The traffic office dashed off a new vehicle registration book by laser printer while we watched and the number-plates were already made and waiting. The whole thing took a couple of minutes and no money changed hands, which is where in Britain the whole system would collapse. In Switzerland everyone is registered and cannot escape when the bill arrives a couple of weeks later.

NOVEMBER 9th:

Zurich's 'Needle Park', once nice gardens by the river and now a no-go area for anyone except drug addicts, has come in for increasing criticism from many quarters. So too has the associated proliferation of petty crime and beggars in the town. The park is an eyesore and every week people die there, either addicts who overdose or dealers who get into fights.

It is unclear what the authorities expected when they started their policy of free needles, but this and their seemingly liberal policy on drug taking has attracted every addict and his dog from the whole of Switzerland and beyond. Only 20% of the people in the park come from the town of Zurich. This has been the subject of fierce debate and now Zurich council have agreed to try and clear it up. The question now is where will all these people go? Most people say "NIMBY" (not in my back yard).

NOVEMBER 23rd:

Regula's family had a get-together. We met in East Switzerland in a museum which was opened that afternoon especially for us. Why a museum? Well, the building that now houses the museum was Regula's great grandparents' house until 1905. After the museum, which is dedicated to local life in the last century, we proceeded to a hostelry for the customary feeding. Thirty-five relations were there, including some of the more elderly and eccentric. Like an uncle who dislikes dentists, so he has never been to one in his life. At age eighty-nine he still has one tooth left (central eating). He speaks German, French, Italian, Latin, Greek, Hebrew and of course English, the trouble is nobody can tell the difference without his teeth.

Another uncle, Robert, a retired doctor and pushing eighty-eight could enter the Guiness Book of Records with the length of his eyebrows and his speeches. He was recently having dinner with Regula's parents and they were discussing of all things, the number of cabins on the giant wheel at the fair that is on in the middle of Zurich at the moment. They all had different ideas as to how many there were. He was so sure his estimate of the number was right that at 10 pm, instead of taking the train home, he went in the opposite direction, to the fair ground. With walking stick and eyebrows amid the bustling night-time crowd, he counted the cabins on the wheel. He was right.

DECEMBER 2nd:

I have long ago abandoned any ideas of learning German. Who heard of a British tourist who could speak a word of it? I find by living here, I am very slowly learning a bit without trying, but not much.

The English language often reflects the British class system. In German people who work for a company are called *Mitarbeiter* which means literally 'with-workers'. In English this is 'staff' or 'employees', which means that they are below the level of employers, rather than working with them. I spotted some crusty bread in the supermarket called *Handwerkerbrot,* even in French it sounded quite dignified as *Pain d' Artisan.* Both much better than 'Manual Worker's Bread'. But English does win sometimes. 'Schadenfreude' appears in the Oxford Dictionary. It means malicious enjoyment at another's downfall and it shows what nice people we are, as we have no word for it in English.

The Swiss love the English language particularly in advertising and the names of hairdressers' shops. It is the fashion to wear clothes with English printed on them. Much of this is produced in the Far East and Switzerland seems to have become a dumping ground for garments with nonsensical English on them. After the discovery of Swinglish comes another language: 'T-shirt English'. I saw a big pot-bellied, middle-aged man sporting a brand-new white sweat shirt with " P R E T T Y   B O Y " emblazoned across his chest in huge red letters.

DECEMBER 14th:

Regula's brother, Andreas, bought a video camera some months ago and in conversation mentioned that he didn't find it very convenient to use as they do not have a video recorder on which to play their recordings back. I asked why he didn't play the camera back directly through the TV. He said their TV was too old. Tentatively I asked how exactly he and his family enjoyed the happy hours of home entertainment they had made. It appears they had been taking turns watching with one eye through the black and white viewfinder of the camera, without sound.

I tried to get the camera to playback through their TV and, after a few false starts, it worked. They sat down to watch in colour and sound for the first time and were very pleased. And to think I let this man take blood from me.

We know what to buy Andreas and his family for Christmas because they only have one video cassette, the one supplied free with the camera. Their elder son Raphael, aged fifteen, borrowed the camera some weeks ago and had not revealed what for. But the camera cannot lie. He had gone with a school friend to a lonely high bridge over a deep ravine to try out their climbing equipment. His parents watched in silent horror as he swung recklessly 25 metres (75ft) above the rocky ground. Then Raphael and their camera abseiled to the wildly rushing river below. And my parents used to worry about me! (By the way, *abseilen* is the German to 'down rope'.)

DECEMBER 18th:

According to a READERS' DIGEST survey of TV watching in Europe, the Swiss watch the least, averaging 11.86 hours per week, and the British the most at 20.74 hours. Regula said it showed how intelligent the Swiss are. I said it showed how lousy Swiss TV is – there is no James Bond film on Christmas Day for a start. A BBC TV and Radio Times survey found that 80% of the British watched TV on Christmas Day and 33% even watched it while eating Christmas lunch. I imagine a fair few watch it while asleep too.

DECEMBER 24th:

We are spending Christmas in Switzerland and have bought a tree. Trees are sold in every town, in squares and open places, by authorised Christmas tree vendors with a valid permit. What happens to the trees at night? Are they taken back to a warehouse to prevent the trees, which sell from Sfr 15 to Sfr 100 each, from being stolen? No, the trees are put into neat heaps and left in the open. Are they still there next morning? Of course they are!

DECEMBER 30th:

Regula's sister Vroni has two children, Sami, now five, and Nicola, aged three, who can be a bit of a handful. They both stayed overnight at Regula's parents who babysat them. Vroni said the kids did not like frankfurters, but when they spotted one in the fridge they decided they both wanted it. It was the only one in the house and their grandmother suggested cutting it in two. This did not go down too well with Sami, who fancied all of it and likes to get his own way. He took his little sister out of the kitchen to discuss the matter further. A few minutes later she returned all smiles to declare that Sami had made her an offer that she couldn't refuse. "Don't worry, Gran. Sami says if he can have the whole sausage tonight, I can have it tomorrow!"

JANUARY 1st:

Many of my students have told me they always watch a film called *Dinner for One* on TV every New Year's Eve. It is an institution in German-speaking countries. It was described to me as an old British comedy with a famous English actor playing a butler. This time we watched it.

It is an old black and white twenty-minute sketch starring, not Sir Alec Guiness, as some students had thought, but the now-deceased Lancashire comedian Freddie Frinton whose speciality was to play a drunk. I saw him in a Christmas pantomime in Lancashire years ago.

In *Dinner for One* he plays a butler who has to make the toasts for guests no longer present at an old lady's party. With each glass, he gets progressively more pickled and asks: "Same procedure as last year M'Lady?" and she replies "The same procedure as every year." I have never seen it before and it is unknown in Britain.

It is rather like reversed Swiss roll, if you see what I mean. Swiss roll is a bland sponge and jam cake that the British scoff by the million. No one in Switzerland has ever heard of Swiss roll, but I still ask everyone I meet.

JANUARY 4th:

Every twelve months my residents' permit needs renewing and I receive a form to fill in from the community office. My employers have to countersign and stamp the form and I have to pay Sfr 54 for another year. I work with four English colleagues, but none of them has to do this. The reason is they are women and have both Swiss and British nationality. They got their Swiss nationality by saying *ja* to the question: Do you take this man?

This year sees a change in Swiss law for foreigners married to Swiss partners. Originally it favoured Swiss men, who could automatically endow Swiss nationality upon their foreign wives, like my English teacher colleagues. Swiss women, like Regula, could not reciprocate for their foreign husbands. The playing field has been levelled so that neither Swiss men nor women can automatically bestow citizenship on their partners.

From now on, foreign men and women who have lived in Switzerland for five years and have been married to a Swiss for three years can get Swiss nationality for Sfr 300 plus administration costs. Still longer and more expensive than just saying *ja*, but not bad for lifetime membership of one of the world's most exclusive clubs. In a couple of years I will be eligible. The permit business will end, I can actually own property here, if I could afford it, and leave the country for more than six months without having to reapply to come back.

The Swiss are rather pleased that two of their nearest neighbours, Germany and Austria who have a lot of people living here, do not permit their nationals to have more than one nationality. The hope is these foreigners will want to stay foreign. Good old Blighty allows dual nationality, I just hope the Swiss will eventually accept this tourist as a citizen.

JANUARY 6th:

Regula started her new job with a large multinational insurance company. The first day she attended an introductory seminar with thirty others starting at the same time. They were shown the company's facilities, like the swimming pool. The job seems fine, but even with flexi-time the latest start is 8.30 am, so we have to get up earlier again.

JANUARY 13th:

An ageing rock guitarist interviewed on TV, Ozzy Wasgood or some such, said he was still able to hear because he always wore earplugs when he played. But many of his contemporaries were seriously deaf. He strongly recommended that all rock musicians and their audiences wear earplugs. This is all very fine, but wouldn't it be much simpler if they just turned the volume down. Pardon?

JANUARY 24th:

Our car is serviced by the little man we bought our first one from. He works under a block of flats in Regula's parents' road. What a funny and complicated chap he can be. He is an Austrian called Herr Wanzenböck and whenever I try to book in the car it is a major event. He always says it is impossible for him to do anything as he is so busy. I reply that the service is not urgent and I can leave the car with him all week. He says he has not got the space to keep cars, but if I bring the car the next day he will see what he can do, but he makes no promises.

Next day at 5 pm, when I phone to see if he has finished, he does not answer. He never answers the phone. I have to ask Regula's father if he can pop over and check. Her father then phones me back to say that the car is finished and I must come at once as Wanzenböck is complaining that it is in his way. I rush over there on the tram only to find that Wanzenböck has gone. On his locked door he has left a little scrap of paper saying he will be back in half an hour.

When Wanzenböck returns, he does not look at me but grunts a greeting and goes on doing something else for a few minutes. Then he slowly warms to my presence and starts talking. I can never simply get the bill and go. First he opens his dustbin to show me all the old parts he has replaced in the service – spark plugs and oil filter and so on. He slides under the car and starts pulling at bits and tapping things. Then he beckons me to accompany him under the bonnet for a guided tour of the engine.

He wiggles cables and taps metal pipes with his spanner. After that comes his tour de force. Out comes his can of GUNK ENGINEBRITE and he sprays the rubber hoses and makes them shine. A few more tugs at the battery leads and he wanders off to find the empty cans of oil he has used for the engine. Having found them, he holds the cans upside-down over his head to demonstrate that he has done the impossible and cheated the oil companies by getting out every drop. He triumphantly lets me in on his secret, which I am privileged to pass on to you: the cans have to stay upside-down over the oil filler hole all day to get all the oil out.

Next comes the hardest part for Herr Wanzenböck – the bill. He is a strictly cash-only man, and has a large sign stating this hanging in his workshop. He collects together odd scraps of grubby grease-stained telephone message pads and jots down odd figures with a biro that does not work properly. After much mental arithmetic he always arrives at a figure of Sfr 250. This he firmly states is for parts only and his valuable time must be added.

The grand total is Sfr 350. This is a very tricky juncture in the proceedings, if I falter at this stage I will be led back to the car to be shown the shiny engine again. Thence on to the oil cans and finally the rubbish bin of replaced parts. I must quickly whip out my wallet and pay him or spend another fifteen minutes being shown my car. At the sight of money he smiles for the first time. As I get into the car, he attempts to clean the windscreen with an oily rag. Finally, he can be seen in my mirror, waving like a long-lost relative, as I pull away.

FEBRUARY 4th:

Regula is now settling into her new job. It is a bit of a culture shock for her. Before she was top of a very little heap and could please herself what she did, now she is a small cog in a big wheel.

Speaking of sprockets, a man from Birmingham phoned up the other day and Regula answered. He said his name was "Koyth" she asked him again and this time he said it slower – "Koy-ith", eventually he had to spell it – K e i t h – a tourist and no mistake.

FEBRUARY 8th:

Zurich council have closed down the notorious 'Needle Park'. They have also, at a cost of Sfr 2 million per year, started the night-time closing of the central station and underground shopping area, where the dropouts used to drop out. A private security police force has been employed to do this and clear the streets of people begging. The addicts are going to go elsewhere. The question is where? As long as it is not near where we live – NIMBY now stands for 'No Injections Means Begging Youths'.

FEBRUARY 11th:

The next visit to the Swiss ballot box includes a very emotive proposition to stop experiments on animals. More money is being spent advertising both for and against vivisection than any other issue I have seen. It is an ideal subject for publicity purposes, with grizzly pictures of cats and dogs being operated on. It is a medical subject and the layman is not in a position to know whether these experiments are necessary. The sooner the publicity campaigns are over the better it will be for tourists to walk the streets.

There is also a proposal to subsidise private health insurance funds with government money and make a partial national-health service. Due to the all-too-familiar spiralling increases in the cost of medical treatment, our health insurance went up 15% this year. If I know the Swiss, the proposal will be rejected. The Swiss public have realised one thing which the British still find very hard to understand; there is simply no such thing as 'the government paying'. No government has any funds of its own, it collects its money from the likes of you and me. To pay for any subsidising of health care would mean extra taxes.

On the subject of health, an item on the Swiss TV news today was about the first Swiss person to reach 110 (years old, not kilometres per hour on the crowded roads). They will all want to do it now. She was originally French, but has lived in Switzerland for at least the 20th century. She came down the stairs of her home on the arm of her son to face the TV cameras. Her son, by the way, is eighty-five!

FEBRUARY 13th:

The Swiss have been so impressed with the way their tunnelling machines dug the Channel Tunnel only six months behind schedule, that some bright spark has come up with the idea of a 'Swiss Metro'. This would be a high speed underground rail system that would cross the country north to south and east to west beneath the Alps and forests and out of sight of all objectors. With speeds of up to 500kph (300mph), it would take forty-five minutes to get from the German border to Italy. It would also blow your hat off if you stood too close and blow your mind if you knew the cost.

The underground would comply with the Swiss ideals of keeping noise and pollution to an absolute minimum while at the same time costing a fortune. Since there are objections to the high-speed rail link from the Channel Tunnel to London from the NIMBY crowd (this time = Not In Middle-England Better in Yorkshire), the Chunnel could be extended to London. It would be called the 'Chundon' and be ready by the year 3000.

FEBRUARY 16th – 23rd:

We had a great week skiing, this time in Valbella Lenzerheide. On a previous ski holiday I was reminded of my age by a Canadian who was born two years after I visited his home city of Montreal. This time our ski instructor said that his parents were coming to visit for a few days. I imagined a grey-haired couple from the MOGADON generation who would be barely capable of a light stroll round the lake after their SANATIGEN and afternoon nap. You can picture my shock to find that they were my age and skied in our class.

We experienced our first earthquake while we were in Lenzerheide. I'll try anything once. At dinner in our hotel there was a loud crash sounding like a fight breaking out in the kitchens. The sound came simultaneously with a short sharp vibration. It lasted no more than two seconds. I thought it was an explosion, but the sound and vibration together puzzled me. The electricity was unaffected and nobody took much notice of it. From the news the next morning, we learned it was an earthquake.

MARCH 27th:

The sensible Swiss voters said 'no' to a national health system. They also rejected by a small margin the proposal to stop experiments on animals, obviously not a nation of animal lovers this.

But they are very concerned about the ozone hole. Switzerland is doing its bit to stop that hole getting bigger. Purchasers of new fridges and freezers must buy a Sfr 69 voucher at the same time as their new appliance. The voucher is for the cost of correctly disposing of the old fridge and its nasty ozone-eating freon. You cannot buy a new fridge without buying a voucher. This makes the assumption that every household in Switzerland already has a fridge and a freezer to be disposed of.

APRIL 1st:

Satellite TV, some of which is pumped through our cable system, has brought a new lease of life to direct selling of goods that "are not available in any shops." (One is tempted to ask why they are not.) Hardly a week goes by without some new wonder product being advertised. The latest is the amazing thigh slimmer. These can be ordered by phone in local currencies throughout Europe. £24.99 in Britain, Sfr 75 in Switzerland and an unbelievable 499,000 Zloties in Poland – sounds like a football pools win, but what I want to know is who is going to count it and does this mean the Pope is a millionaire?

Things cannot be too bad: the man from the till in the *Bahnhof Buffet* self-service restaurant has just come back from his customary three weeks in St Lucia.

APRIL 5th:

Each winter I put on 3 kilos and in the spring I diet off 2 kilos. On this projection I should hit 100 kilos in the year 2012. To break the cycle I have been trying the previously recommended banana diet. Eating only bananas and drinking only milk or water. It is very easy and cheap. It is also convenient as bananas are easily carried on one's person, unlike the equipment required for a pineapple diet. After four days I have lost about 2.5 kilos, but mainly from my face. While I ate bananas I was not hungry, but now I have stopped I am unbelievably hungry. The result is that I am eating more than ever now.

APRIL 9th:

Now for some jollier news: our landlords' cat has been run over by a car. Their daughter came to tell us amid sobs this morning at about 7.45 am. This was just as Regula was entering her final blind panic phase of getting ready for work. After Regula had charged off up the road in the direction of the tram stop, I went downstairs to see the Müllers. I thought perhaps the children were there by themselves and I ought to bury the cat for them. But the whole family was there, all watery eyed, which was for the best as I later discovered that it is forbidden to bury dead pets yourself. They have to be collected by, or delivered to, the dead pets' police, who dispose of them in a hygienic manner for an appropriate fee.

Why can't one bury dead pets in Swiss gardens? It is considered that rotting pets can harm the ground water and thus the drinking water supply. And that Mark (of ski accident fame) had the cheek to ask if it was all right to drink the tap water when he first came to Zurich.

APRIL 13th

The Swiss are always shaking hands. When they meet and when they part. Even the children do it. It is not unusual, when a group of half a dozen fourteen-year-old school children meet in the street, to see the boys shaking hands. The girls kiss each other on the cheeks and better still the boys get to kiss the girls. There is, though, some sort of protocol to be followed, because one has to remember who one is on kissing terms with and who one is not.

It is the same in Britain, but what is different is the number of kisses to be administered at any one session. The British and Commonwealth average is a modest one kiss. The mature German-speaking Swiss go for two. While the French-speaking and the younger generation of German-speaking Swiss will have kissed you three times before you have had a chance to pull away.

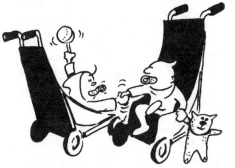

Etiquette for English speakers is easy with our one form of 'you'. *Sie* (the German formal and plural form of you) and *du* (the familiar form of you) is causing Regula some trouble at her new job. It is a big company and she has contact with a lot of people and must remember who to call *du* and who to call *Sie*. It is very rude to get it wrong either way. The British living in Switzerland make a not very funny joke of it by saying "you can call me you".

Du and *Sie* are as incomprehensible for the English-speaker to have, as for the German-speaker not to have. I have been asked a number of times by mystified students if there is anything different in the 'you' we use with our parents and the 'you' we use with, say, the butcher. When I say there is none at all, the confusion rises further. It is then suggested that I must pronounce 'you' in a different way to these two parties. An earnest question posed with such conviction that, when first asked, I actually mouthed "you" a couple of times before answering no.

Regula is sure that my misunderstanding of the significance of these two forms and, equally important, who should decide to change from *Sie* to *du* nearly cost us our flat. Before moving to Switzerland, we flew out from England to see the flat. We spent a pleasant hour with our landlords-to-be, the Müllers, who are about our age. A couple of bottles of rather pleasant white wine were sunk in their company. As we were going they shook hands and said in English, "Goodbye Mr Bilton and Goodbye Mrs Bilton." To British ears this was very strange, not to say downright odd. Like a prize tourist, I said without a thought for the consequences: "Oh, call me Paul!" This put them in a difficult situation and made them divulge their Christian names. Worse it left us still saying *Sie* to one another, but using first names. My social gaffe could not be corrected until after we moved in. When, following the established protocol, *Duzis* was officially made. This has to be done with a glass or three of wine.

APRIL 17th to 25th:

We spent Easter in England. The weather was diabolical and I managed to keep off the subject of my cholesterol level. This time, I am sorry to say, I noticed that most English people were very polite. I hardly bumped into anyone the whole time I was in England and nobody bumped into me. Some Swiss people seem to have no concern about others in public places and are always colliding into one another. In England I held open shop doors for people and they smiled and said thank you. When I do that in Zurich I am either ignored or stared at as though I am mad. The lack of smoking-associated coughing and spitting, was also much appreciated in England.

Regula does not have a British passport. Long ago I asked her if she wanted one, she replied "why?" and that was the end of the conversation. The only disadvantage would be when we came into Britain together. I follow the 'British and EU passports' channel and she should queue up to be quizzed with 'all other passports'. However, we have found that we can go together through the Brit and EU channel. I ask "Is it all right if my wife comes through with me?" and a smiling face says "Of course, sir!"

Swiss who go to Britain complain at the intense questioning they receive at the immigration desk on arrival. They point out that I don't have the same treatment when I arrive in Switzerland. It's true. But in Britain there is no registration of inhabitants. When you move house in Britain, there is no need to inform any authority, you just go. Once in Britain, it would be possible for Swiss people to live there undetected and perhaps work. However with 11% unemployment, pay-levels a third of those in Switzerland and taxes double, this seems an unlikely scenario. The British immigration officer is doing the work of the Swiss foreign police and community office.

We spotted a new craze at English supermarket-checkouts. Every time a ten-pound note (Sfr 25) or higher was tendered as payment, the note was carefully scrutinised by the checkout girls. This included holding them up to the light and feeling the paper to see if they were genuine. In larger establishments, with thirty or more checkouts, there was almost continuous banknote wafting over the cash-tills. No forgeries were found, but maybe that was the idea. These theatrics were guaranteed to put off potential crooks using their home-made money.

In England I had to concentrate on driving on the left for the first time. My countrymen and women are starting to look a little pale and rundown, but they are still jolly and as optimistic as ever. Maybe this impression is only in contrast to the high gloss and stiff faces of Zurich's Bahnhofstrasse. Sadly as soon as we got back to Zurich airport, the politeness was gone. We called a lift for the car park and when it arrived we let some Swiss people in it first with their luggage trolley. Once inside the lift, they stood in the way and ignored us, talking among themselves. One of them eventually noticed me when I pushed our trolley into her ankles and she said "Ow!" Regula asked them for the sixth floor, they pressed the button for the ninth floor. When we arrived up on the ninth floor, we had to get out first to let them out. Did they say "thank you"? Not a word from them. But Regula made her feelings known through the closing doors as we were back on our way down to the sixth floor.

MAY 4th:

The Swiss are still being rude to me, perhaps I am being too English. I was boarding a tram with some of my students after school. The front door of Zurich trams is opened from the inside and not the outside like the other doors. We approached the tram from the front and a passenger got out of this front door, so as it was open we started to board through it.

The driver was changing shifts and his replacement was behind me waiting to get on through the front door too. The driver got out of his cab and wanted to come down the steps, so I stood back and waited for him. Instead of getting off he shouted, so that all of the tram could hear, that the tram had other doors and refused to move until I went away to one of them. This I did but not before I had recalled one of my favourite expressions – "Who's the customer?" I even surprised myself by asking this in German. It, alas, did not impress him. If I had played the perpetual tourist and spoken to him in English he would have probably stepped back and let me on board.

MAY 8th:

Summer weather is slowly slipping in and we managed a fifteen-kilo-metre walk along the length of the Walensee. A lake with steep sides where

William Tell did not do his stuff. We were surprised to hear laughter and animated conversation as we rounded a quiet bend on the wooded path. It was not a demented walker talking to himself, but a walker on his mobile phone. He was wishing the person on the other end a happy birthday. I then tripped over a manhole cover. The Swiss Alps are full of manhole covers. I suspect that every mountain is plumbed for hot and cold.

MAY 14th:

Zurich public transport system and a local newspaper have got together with a number of sponsors to provide 100 bicycles for people to use free-of-charge. These bikes are no old rubbish pulled out of the lake either, although there would be more than enough machines from that source. They are brand-new twenty-one gear city bikes and are publicised under the suitably Swiss slogan 'I like Züri-Bike'. You just deposit your ID (or passport if you are a tourist) and off you pedal for the day.

MAY 17th:

Amongst the items to be decided next time the Swiss bash the ballot is an initiative to stop further development of water power. Because so many rivers and lakes have been altered to make reservoirs the proposal claims enough is now enough. However the electricity-generating authorities say there will not be enough power if development is restricted. Nuclear power development was voted to a ten-year halt a number of votes ago. At this rate they are going to have to start looking for coal soon, until someone objects to that too.

MAY 21st:

A student had a problem with a question from a past Cambridge Certificate English Exam paper which went like this: *Re-write this sentence to mean exactly the same, starting as shown: 'Susan is the tallest girl in her class.' Starting: Nobody...* The answer should be 'Nobody in Susan's class is taller than her.' My student's attempt was "Nobody among the girls in Susan's class is taller than her, but some of the boys probably are, in fact I think quite a lot must be, they certainly were in my class." The problem lay in the Swiss coeducation system. My student assumed that Susan must be in a mixed class of boys and girls, not in a British single-sex school. He thought that the first sentence meant she was the tallest of the girls, but there would be boys who were probably taller than her. He went on to pass the First Certificate, but only after some Swiss logic had been knocked out of him.

Another student visited London and reported how clean she found the city. I queried this remembering my countrymen and their casual attitudes to life in general and rubbish in particular. She said there was no graffiti in London. In Zurich and other Swiss towns graffiti is a big problem. Nearly every building has some graffiti, which varies from mindlessly sprayed initials to major works of art. A Zurich property owner has found a way to beat the sprayers; when his house was recently repainted he commissioned an artist to spray graffiti round the building. It looks bizarre, but there is no room for any less-artistic or obscene graffiti now. My student asked if the British have more respect for their buildings than the Swiss. The answer is that potential British sprayers simply could not afford to buy the amount of aerosols needed for a good graffit.

On the subject of writing on the wall: Look & Learn, the first school with the foresight to employ me, will shortly be looking and learning no longer. Having staggered on in difficult trading conditions and with few students, the owners have decided the school will close at the end of June. They hoped it was not too much of a surprise for me. I said the surprise was that they had managed to keep going for so long. There has been little improvement in the hours I do there since I started three years ago. I was going to ask them for a rise, but I shall skip it now.

MAY 23rd:

My bank in England will be pleased to learn that Swiss banks also make mistakes. On my last statement there was an item of Sfr 5 for "instructions by telex". We looked high and low and I was right – we don't have a telex machine. I queried the amount and the bank replied saying what a fool their computer was and credited the Sfr 5.

The Swiss are throwing their campaign for European Union membership into top gear. Suddenly there is a blind panic to get into 'Europe' as quickly as possible. Why this should be is a mystery to me. If something has worked well for over 700 years why change it? I guess it is the Swiss lack of self-confidence that has given them the jitters.

Switzerland is experiencing a recession, although to the eye of a tourist all seems as well as ever. The Swiss feel that they are alone on an economic island in the middle of the continent. They fear that somebody is making a better club than theirs, and everything that the Swiss have worked for over many years will be whipped away from under their feet. Very odd.

There will be a vote in December on joining the European Economic

Area – a sort of wider Europe that Switzerland has the opportunity to join along with other EFTA (European Free Trade Association) members. If this first step is accepted, full EU membership could follow within four years. No doubt Switzerland would be welcomed with open arms as a rich new member to help with the EU finances. Switzerland's isolation would go and with it perhaps the high standard of living. Having vowed over 700 years ago not to be ruled by any other than a fellow countryman, the Swiss seem suddenly willing to break that vow and seek rule from Brussels.

MAY 25th:

The Swiss Telephone Company (the PTT – still part of the post office and still nationalised) started a system where companies and individuals can offer services and party-lines on phone numbers prefixed with 156. We are not talking about weather forecasts or cricket test-match scores. Names like 'Bruno's Gay Box' and 'Live Sex' tell it all. There is a full page of ads for these phone numbers in the paper, each making wilder and filthier claims about what you can hear when you phone at a cost of between Sfr 1.40 and 2.00 per minute. The lines are jammed with kinky callers (this is what I have been told, not experienced). The un-kinky part of Switzerland are up in arms about it. About half of Switzerland is kinky by the way. A recent TV documentary revealed that one evening's phoning could cost Sfr 500 and one rather fat chatter's two-months' bill was a staggering Sfr 15,000! If anyone starts up an English conversation party line on a 156 number, you can tell them that I thought of it first.

MAY 28th:

Today is Ascension Day and, like Whit Monday, is a public holiday in Switzerland and the funny old-fashioned Swiss still celebrate these holidays on the actual days, a practice long since abandoned in the UK, where May 1st, for example, is obstinately celebrated on the first Monday after May 1st (except of course when May 1st is a Monday). This is with good reason, for the British have proved themselves incapable of taking a one-day public holiday on any other day but a Monday or Friday. Otherwise the holidays are unofficially extended to include the nearest weekend. Should the holiday fall on a Wednesday, the British would include both the previous and the next weekend, thus extending their one day's holiday into a ten-day break.

JUNE 1st:

A colleague who works at the soon-to-be-disbanded Look & Learn language school went for a job interview with the Swiss civil service. She had to take a certificate from the police to say that she had no criminal record. These are available from police stations throughout Switzerland at Sfr 15 each. If I ever return to live in England, I will get one of these certificates and have it framed for the lounge wall, providing of course, that I remain on the right side of the law.

Last summer the speed limits were reduced on the Swiss autobahns to cut down on smog. It is unclear whether it improved the air, but the lower speed limits did reduce accidents. If the government are interested in saving lives they should do it again, or even lower the speed limit permanently. However, lives lost in accidents do not seem to be important and it is only the air quality that the Swiss care about. This year the authorities have side-stepped the whole issue of speed limits. Instead they have raised the minimum danger levels for smog and other noxious gases. These new higher levels will not be reached and there is now no need to reduce the speed limits.

JUNE 5th:

The Swiss always like to talk and debate new ideas and proposals, but I have realised that many of the things that have been agreed take a long time to come into force. For instance a year ago a ban on amusement arcades in the Canton of Zurich was agreed by vote. Despite being passed by the people, the arcades remain open and more have opened since the vote. The owners of the arcades have taken the matter to court in protest. The Canton receives an income from the arcades in tax, so there is no pressure to implement the vote. Remember the graffiti "If voting really made a difference they wouldn't let us"? An earlier vote approved the completion of the autobahn system, including the autobahn ring round the town of Zurich. Because of a lack of political will, nothing will be started until at least five years after the voters said 'yes'.

We had our own vote before we decided to pay Sfr 150 each for a *Halbtaxabo*. This is a yearly ticket that will allow us to travel on the Swiss railways and most other public transport at half price. We have also joined Regula's company sports club. They go everywhere by train, so we should get our investment back within a few months. We can buy the half price train tickets with REKA CHECKS, which are a kind of travellers' cheque, that Regula buys from her company at a discount of 20%. The Sports Club refund us 35% of the price of the train tickets when we travel with them, which is the way the Swiss love to do things, i.e. paying as little as possible. By my calculations, if we are not careful we will be paid for travelling by train.

JUNE 8th:

Zurich's permanently-under-reconstruction main station is now in its eleventh year of alterations with no end in sight. There is a whole generation of Zurich children growing up who believe a railway station is a place for trains and mechanical diggers. Amid all the upheaval they have opened a *Rösti* bar. There are ten different kinds of *Rösti* available and we popped in there today. It is Switzerland's answer to fast food and is a sort of cross between a McDonald's and a McDonald's.

JUNE 30th:

The Look & Learn language school has now officially sunk without trace. We celebrated with a sort of 'Titanic' meal out, financed by the remains of the petty cash. It was the school that gave me my first break, and now they are broke.

JULY 11th – AUGUST 1st:

All thoughts of teaching were put aside as we spent three weeks in the Western States of America. What did we like best as tourists in the land of tourists? National parks, oldies radio stations, orange juice, prices (which were generally half those of Switzerland), the courteous relaxed driving in the US and the lack of smoking.

Dislikes must include American food, which is strangely sweet and served in huge portions, coffee, which is like hot tinted-water and tap water which tastes as though it is straight out of a swimming pool. My other dislike was queuing up at restaurants when there were unoccupied tables.

The relationship between the Americans and the English is like that between the German-speaking Swiss and the Germans. The English have watched American TV for the last forty years. American names such as Roy Rogers, Rin-Tin-Tin, Rowan and Martin, Mr Magoo and Mr Ed are all familiar to the British. 50 per cent of Britain's TV is American, in the original American English. What has this done for the British nation, other than soften their brains? The English, like the Swiss with the Germans, understand everything Americans say. But Americans appear to be at a loss when it comes to spotting a Brit, let alone understanding one. Presenting my Swiss driving licence in America when cashing travellers' cheques would evoke gracious compliments on my grasp of English. Once I was asked if I was from Scandinavia or Australia, two areas apparently close together in American geography.

The misunderstandings were not all one way. Regula thought that 'Kids Free' on a large illuminated sign outside a motel must mean free of kids and so there would be no children in the motel! We kept seeing 'HBO' advertised outside motels. We discovered this was Home Box Office, America's biggest cable TV company, so big that it makes its own movies.

This brings up the whole sorry subject of American television, once noted for there being a lot of it, though bland and trivial. Now there is much more of it, the bland has gone and violence has replaced it. The cable system seems to be uncensored. In any other society this would result in nonstop sex on TV. However, America is where a bikini on the beach is risqué and topless is unthinkable and the land where they go to the bathroom because they can't say toilet. But blowing heads off people can be seen every three minutes on TV. Documentaries are shown as long as they were devoted to the killing power of the shark.

We had no idea what channel we were watching. One motel boasted forty-five channels, but they could not provide me with a list of which channel was what. The owner said they only ever watched HBO themselves.

Americans are not prepared for British humour. Like the man in a visitor centre who sat beneath a plastic three-dimensional map of the Death Valley area. The place where the centre was had been fingered so much that the plastic had cracked revealing the black wall underneath. I asked him if the crack in the map was the San Andreas Fault. He earnestly pointed out the correct position of the fault which was much further south. Regula then chipped in and asked him if the coloured pin in the top of the map holding it to the wall was to show where we were.

I had hoped to solve two great mysteries of the American way of life as always portrayed by Hollywood in films and TV series. How is it that Americans are always able to stand under a shower, turn it on and never get a shot of cold water first? And equally mystifying, do Americans really never say 'goodbye' on the phone and simply hang up when they have finished like in every movie?

The shower business remains a mystery. Every shower I tried the water was cold for the first fifteen seconds. The phoney goodbye also remains unsolved. The reason is that the American phone system, like their TV, is now a wild deregulated monster running out of control. We attempted to make six phone calls in America. None was straightforward and only two calls got through and then I was so surprised that I forgot to say goodbye. Maybe that's the reason they don't say it either.

For an Englishman a visit to the USA would not be complete without a few great Americanisms. Like the preposterous English we heard from a Ranger in a national park who blurted out "The rate of visitations at this location is, at this moment in time, on an upward curve." I think he meant that more people were coming to the park, rather than that it was haunted. They have some wonderful expressions like "to chill out" (to cool down or calm down a lot) or "it'll blow you away", which I think means that it will be a bit of a surprise. How can I explain to students the short-form of English we saw in huge letters on a billboard advertising a restaurant? It provocatively posed the mouth-watering challenge – "Wanna Dine?"

Americans say "dove" (like in the British town Dover, not dove the bird) for the past of to dive. Thus "I hit my head when I dived in the swimming baths" becomes in American English; "I received multiple contusions to the cranial region when I dove in the pool and my lawyers are on the case at this time."

Hankering after Swiss-style coffee instead the brown water, one evening in a restaurant I enquired whether espresso or cappuccino were available. The waitress looked perplexed and after a moment's thought she replied tentatively "Say, is that some kind of *carfee?*" Regula soon got tired of repeating "coffee" two or three times each time she replied to the question "tea or *carfee?*" and started replying *carfee*. The same happened with salad dressings. She preferred ranch dressing and she soon resorted to pronouncing it *rernch*, which was understood at once.

At times it was hard to see where Disneyland ended and America began. We stayed one night in a ridiculous motel built like a castle with a heart-shaped Jacuzzi in every bedroom. The Jacuzzi took about 200 gallons (900 litres) of water to fill. In the same room was a card explaining that iced water was not served at their restaurant in order to save water. Which brings up the sorry subject of America and the environment. From water saving to energy saving, they appear to be on another planet, certainly not the planet that includes Switzerland. Any Swiss motorist who is worried about the effects of using his car too much should see the five solid lanes of traffic in each direction on the LA freeway system.

The American principle of 'big is beautiful' appears as strong as ever. From the outsized portions served in restaurants to the outsized people who eat those portions. Even the toilet paper in motel rooms boasted 1000 sheets per roll. But to achieve this number per roll meant that the sheets were so thin that you could read a newspaper through them.

Despite thin toilet paper, odd English and watery coffee, we had an excellent holiday and hope to return to America before too long.

AUGUST 4th:

Back in small, tidy Switzerland we are trying to return to a state of what the Americans would call 'normalcy', both in our eating habits and English language speaking. We are jet-lagged and wake up in the early hours expecting steak and are near collapse by 4 o'clock in the afternoon. After being referred to as "you guys", as in "Whatchu guys wanna order?" in American restaurants, it is nice to be back to some kind of sanity. Yet the only time in our whole US trip that we found pedestrians blocking our way was in Santa Monica: they turned out to be a crowd of Swiss.

AUGUST 7th:

It's Quiz Time. How many umbrellas are left on Zurich's public transport system during a year? Can you guess? Answer later on.

I don't have much luck with silencers on my cars. The silencer blew on my latest car and I had to have it replaced. It cost Sfr 640. This is 10% of what we paid for the whole car. Appropriately the job was done by Midas Silencers, named after the mythical king who turned rusty silencers into gold.

Swiss summer weather is generally hot and humid, which is a great mystery to the English whose favourite question to me about living in Switzerland is "how do you get on with all that snow?" The Swiss on the other hand have trouble with the statistics that prove Zurich has nearly double the rainfall at 1092mm than London at 585mm.

Despite the rainfall, I managed to get in quite a bit of windsurfing during some fine weather. I store the board in the cellar, hanging it from the ceiling. I have been able to get it in and out by myself without problem for the last three years, but our ever helpful landlord decided I needed a bit of help today. He carried it with me into the cellar. While I started to hang it up, he gave the board a final shove and promptly pushed the front straight out through the glass of the cellar window. I'll be putting it away alone again in future.

AUGUST 13th:

There were 3469 umbrellas left on the buses and trams of Zurich. Wasn't that fun? A few of those were mine and getting them back was no easy matter. Zurich's lost property office, obtusely called the 'found office' in German, files everything lost (or found) by the day and the place it was lost. This plays havoc with us tourist types. Good Heavens! We don't lose things deliberately. I have no idea when and where I lost my umbrellas. Once I had an umbrella and next time it rained I did not have one. In the intervening period I travelled by tram a number of times so I assume I left it on one. In order to stand any hope of recovering anything in Switzerland I must learn to lose things in a more orderly fashion.

But being orderly is not all bad. Regula's sister, Vroni, sent her holiday snapshots off in the post to be developed. Somehow her address got parted from the film on the way to the laboratory in Zurich. The laboratory only knew that the package came via the post office in Uster. They developed the film and sent the pictures back to the post office in Uster with a note asking if the postmen recognised anyone in the pictures. Her pictures were passed among the post office staff. Vroni is a teacher and the father of one of her pupils is a postman at Uster. He thought he recognised her, but was not a hundred per cent sure as she looked a little browner and happier on holiday than at work. He telephoned her and asked if she could call in at the post office. As soon as Vroni walked into the post office, the counter staff, now all familiar with the photographs, recognised her at once and she was greeted like a long lost friend.

AUGUST 18th:

Deaths on the roads of Switzerland are at a forty-year low. No one knows quite why. I blame the air bag myself. These figures could be reduced even further if more Swiss could be encouraged to wear seat belts in their cars. Still on the subject of death; a work colleague of Regula, who was unfit, very stressed and a heavy smoker, had scorned her for telling him off for smoking in her office. He celebrated his birthday on Saturday and died of heart failure on Sunday evening. It had been his thirty-fourth birthday.

AUGUST 29th:

Regula's mother fell rather badly at the station on the way to visit her brother (Uncle Robert of the long eyebrows and long speeches fame). Thankfully nothing was broken, but her knees and forehead were cut. She declined an offer to take her to hospital. Her brother is a retired doctor and his house where he ran his practice is near the station. She had not, though, accounted for his lackadaisical ways. On arrival she discovered that the former doctor did not have a single plaster in the house.

AUGUST 30th:

Uncle Robert and his daughter, Ursle, came to visit us. For reasons that were never really clear to me, Uncle Robert arrived separately by taxi. We wondered why the taxi did not deliver him to the door, but left him halfway down our road. He had written our address down for the taxi driver on a piece of paper. The driver could have had it made up at any chemist's counter and he did very well to even deliver him to Zurich, let alone our street.

SEPTEMBER 3rd:

The Swiss are to vote whether to go ahead with NEAT. I thought Switzerland is already neat enough, but N.E.A.T. (pro. knee-at) stands for New European Alp Transit. The idea is to build two new rail-tunnels through the Alps, each as long as the Channel Tunnel. This is to curb road traffic, and lorries in particular, passing through the country. It would also halve the time by train from Zurich to Milan to two hours. The cost is estimated at 14.9 Billion Francs and it would not be finished until 2010.

SEPTEMBER 10th:

The glorious summer ended abruptly and gave way to winter. Autumn, like spring, somehow seems to have been missed out, maybe that will come next. This is a pity because we are between, as the Americans would say, two visitations from England. Firstly my parents came over to be greeted by torrential rain and cold winds. The only thing to do, other than to hibernate, was to go south of the Alps. This we did and sure enough Ticino (the Italian part) was enjoying a different season, not to mention climate.

SEPTEMBER 18th:

My folks' visit was closely followed by that of my sister, Angie, and her husband. They have already been converted to skiing and now we wanted to get them into mountain walking. The weather was not on our side, but we managed despite.

We had a thoroughly enjoyable time. Like good English tourists, we laughed so much that at times it hurt, the odd thing is we cannot remember about what. They did remarkably well with their walking and we only had to say: "Mark & Maggie did the same walk but of course they are ten years younger" and any mountain was soon conquered.

SEPTEMBER 29th:

The Swiss have cast their ballots and have approved the N.E.A.T. initiative and the spending of 15 Billion Francs (an amount so inaccurate that it has already gone up by 10 Million since being mentioned only four paragraphs ago).

This approval bodes well for the pro-Europe lobby, because N.E.A.T. will be a very expensive present from Switzerland to the EU. Beer Germany sends to Italy and tomatoes the Italians send to the Germans will be transported by lorries which will be 'piggybacked' on special trains through Switzerland, like the Channel Tunnel without a Channel. N.E.A.T. is of little direct advantage to the Swiss other than giving them lots of work digging it and helping perpetuate their mania about the quality of the air.

The next vote is the 'biggie'. When Switzerland votes whether to join the European Economic Area and eventually on to possible full European Union membership. It looks as though the Swiss will vote "We're not sure," as opinion polls show that those for it and those against it are neck and neck.

I still feel they have much more to lose than to gain by joining. Events have proved existing members are not so keen on the EU. The French, a founder of the EU voted "We're only just sure" to the Maastrich Treaty. The Danes voted "No thanks" and were told to think again and came up with "Oh, all right then, but don't ask again." The British government dare not ask, having fallen helplessly out of the bottom of the European Monetary System. In all this confusion it is the Swiss franc that is doing best of all.

Mounting unemployment is shaking Switzerland's already jittery confidence. There would be dancing in the streets in Great Britain if they had Switzerland's still relative low unemployment level of 5%. The British city of Liverpool, near where I was born, has a long-term unemployment level of over 20%. School leavers have no hope of finding a job in Liverpool for the foreseeable future. The Swiss, who thought that unemployment would never be a problem for them, are in sackcloth and ashes. The whole nation has fallen into a helpless manic depression. (They can never see the funny side of anything.)

OCTOBER 15th:

The Swiss debate over the EU is reaching fever pitch, if anything in Switzerland can reach fever pitch. The French-speaking part is all for membership, but the German-speaking part (known to Regula as 'the Swiss part') is divided with the 'noes' ahead by a nose. Although it is the most important vote since we have been here and it has generated endless debate, it has not been the usual advertising windfall for the media. Previous votes have produced millions of francs' worth of advertising for the lucky newspaper and poster site owners. There seems little to say in favour of the EU, so the 'yes' campaign is almost silent. The only rumbling comes from the opponents who have had trouble in coming up with anything more imaginative than "Say no to the EEA and EU."

OCTOBER 23rd:

Regula's parents were looking after Vroni's kids, Sami and Nicola, again. The fact that they were there was not going to stop their grandpa having his usual afternoon nap. He lay down on the bed, took off his watch and gave it to Nicola with instructions that he was not to be wakened until the big hand had moved round to the top. She studied the watch carefully (there were about forty minutes to go) and left the room. But thirty seconds later she burst in again shouting "Wake up Grandpa! It's time to get up!" He had forgotten to explain to her that she should watch the big slow minute hand and not the big fast second hand.

OCTOBER 26th:

How is this for Swiss inflation? I bought some saffron in Migros. When I got home, I found we already had an identical packet in the cupboard. I asked Regula why she had put it on the shopping list and she said she thought the first one would be no good by now and showed me the 'best before date': it must be ten years old. Both cost Sfr 2.00.

OCTOBER 31st:

Swiss country restaurants are called *Beiz*. Pronounced 'bites', it is quite appropriate in English, but no one seems to know why the Swiss say *Beiz*. Usually in a *Beiz* everybody says *Grüetzi* (I greet you) to each other on arrival. *Grüetzi* is the most popular word in Swiss-German and what it means depends on you. If you are Australian it means 'G'day'. If you are American it means 'Hi'. For the Londoner it is 'Watcher Cocker' and for the German Swiss it means *Grüetzi*.

After a walk, we wandered into such a hostelry for a cup of coffee and something sticky. After we had Grüetzied the local farming community and they us, out strode the owner (known as the *Beizer* (bites-er)) who proceeded to come round rather awkwardly and shook every hand in the place – ours included.

NOVEMBER 14th:

The man on the till in the *Bahnhof Buffet* (the one who goes to the Caribbean for his hols) says that he can smell snow in the air. He explained that in England you can smell fog in the air and in Switzerland you can smell snow. I said I was surprised he could smell anything above the unique blend of garlic and cigarette smoke that pervades his establishment.

DECEMBER 6th:

After months of debate, public torture and blood letting, the ever sensible Swiss said "we don't think so, thanks" to going into the European Economic Area, with their pals from the EFTA. The Swiss media and politicians who are for membership, were unable to convince 'Josef public' (also know as 'the man in the Strasse'). The result was close – with the 'no' vote only about a 1% ahead of the 'yes'. The difference was greater by cantonal majorities, which is a strange sort of 'disproportional representation', whereby any national vote must carry a majority of the twenty-three cantons to be passed. The German-speaking cantons said *nein* while the French-speaking ones said *oui*, which has served to deepen the divide between the French speakers, called the Swiss *Romandes*, and the German speakers, called the Swiss. This divide is known as the *Rösti-Graben* as it separates those who eat *Rösti* from those who don't. Somehow it loses its ring when translated into the 'fried-potato ditch'.

Instead of the usual low turnout of vote-numbed Swiss going to the polls, this important issue brought out a respectable 78.3% to cast their ballot. Significantly voting day was December 6th, St Nicholas, when traditionally good boys and girls are rewarded and bad ones punished. Who is who remains to be seen. As they say in some of the narrower valleys, "only time William Tell."

DECEMBER 11th:

If life in the latter part of the twentieth century baffles you at times, as often happens to all good tourists, let me console you with what happened to my mother. For her birthday, my sister bought my mother a clip-on digital alarm. The idea being that my mother could leave something cooking and go and do a bit of gardening with the little alarm clipped to her jacket. When the roast, or whatever, was done to a turn, the alarm would bleep. A week later my mother asked my sister if she could take the alarm back to the shop, as it did not work. Despite spending hours trying and even resorting to reading the instructions (a real sign of desperation), neither of my parents could set the digital readout to anything other than 12:00.

My sister took one look at the alarm and rolled her eyes skyward. She saw the problem and solved it instantly. She handed back the alarm and it worked perfectly. My mother had not removed the adhesive sticker from the face of the alarm on which were printed the figures 12:00!

My young nephews, who proved themselves so admirably on the ski slopes, have a strain of tourist in them it seems. Back in England they went with their boy scout troop on a guided tour of their local police station. The police sergeant, who was showing them round the prison cells, pointed to the beds which were only a couple of centimetres off the ground. He asked the scouts why the beds were like that. The scouts were unaware that most of the occupants of the cells are roaring drunk and the beds are to minimise injury when the drunks fall out. The elder boy, who is rarely short of something to say, and seeing that no one else was going to answer, suggested that it might be so that criminals could "lie low" for a while!

DECEMBER 16th:

The Zurich electricity company (three and half years and I am still waiting for our first power cut) has a policy of encouraging its customers to save electricity. Our bills are always accompanied with useful tips for saving, such as: use more candles, sit in the dark more often, wash in cold water and cut the plugs of your appliances. Each year the bill shows how many units we have used in the current(!) year compared to the previous one.

We saved about 20% when we stopped using the little freezer we picked up second hand a few years ago in England. Though we do not want the freezer, we are reluctant to dispose of it, as this will cost us Sfr 69. However there was one consequence that the electricity company did not consider with their save electricity campaign. It has been so successful and electricity usage has been cut by so much, that they may have to charge their customers more for their electricity because they were so efficient in saving it.

Each year seems to contain a Christmas at the end of it and I find Christmas shopping about as much fun as saving electricity. My brother-in-law Andreas seems to have solved both the present-giving and electricity-saving problems at a stroke. For Christmas last year he kindly bought his father a compact disc of a nice classical piece. Sadly his father didn't have a CD player. So this Christmas the choice of present was easy. After his father had spent a year saving electricity by not playing the CD, Andreas bought him a CD player.

DECEMBER 27th:

It was our turn to spend Christmas in England again and we went just for the weekend. Life seems to go on there as normal, even with the recession and unemployment getting ever deeper and higher. The traditional British Christmas has changed little. Now we fall asleep in front of Indiana Jones, instead of James Bond.

Maybe it is because my British nephews and nieces are getting bigger, but I found the speed and violence with which they opened their presents and destroyed the wrapping paper a shock. Regula's Swiss relations by contrast open their parcels slowly and fold the paper neatly keeping the wrapping and ribbons for next time. But they have to be careful with real candles on the tree.

There was the usual air crash a day or two before we flew and although we arrived at London Heathrow on December 23, or luggage came twenty-four hours later via London Gatwick. British Airways advised us the problem was with baggage sorting at Zurich. But Regula said this was a feeble excuse as it is clearly not possible for the Swiss to make such mistakes.

DECEMBER 28th:

Having never experienced an earthquake until last February in Lenzer-heide, back in Zurich, we had our second earthquake in the space of ten months. We had gone to bed for our first early night in weeks in anticipation of upcoming New Year celebrations and at 10.43 pm there was a short, but very solid shock that rocked our bed, like an explosion with no bang. I thought that the old lady downstairs had fallen out of bed. Regula identified it at once as an earthquake. She is getting an old hand at it now. 4.2 on the Richter scale and centred in the Black Forest region of southern Germany where it no doubt shook a gateau or two.

JANUARY 1st:

The New Year starts the long-heralded *Züri-Sack* scheme for the collection of household rubbish. In case tourists thought they could get away with leaving pirate bags in the street, the authority has written a letter to me in English explaining it all. Accompanying the letter was a brochure, also in English, subtly titled 'Sort or Pay'. This means, if I do not sort out my rubbish, they will sort me out. Printed on recycled paper, the literature speaks of "smart Alecs" who might try to leave out old bags (best place for them, I say). There is even a special 'Sack-o-Phon' (not to be confused with a saxophone) number to call in case I need more information.

We look forward to a new year when May 1st holiday falls on a Saturday, Swiss National Day holiday, August 1st, falls on a Sunday, and Christmas and New Year both fall over weekends. Without a single other day off in lieu, the Swiss will be working like loonies this year, the Rubbish Police included – is this a good time to think like a tourist, or what?

JANUARY 4th:

Petrol should have gone up from Sfr 1.00 to Sfr 1.20 a litre. However, somebody got enough signatures to have a referendum on it and the government must wait for the outcome. This is Swiss democracy in action, but it does bring some problems: the single-minded Swiss who voted *nein* to the European Economic Area are going to have to vote about it again. I presume they will have to vote every year until they vote *ja*. The people of Liechtenstein, who share the same money, postal, phone and voting system as Switzerland, said 'yes' to the European Economic Area. This could be interesting.

JANUARY 15th:

Zurich's town council continue to purge the town of cars. The council have at last decided to put a pedestrian crossing in front of Switzerland's biggest combined-railway-station-and-building-site, sometimes known as the main station. This is to save the confused droves of tourists, who have for years taken their lives in their hands and climbed the barriers and taken on the speeding traffic in order to get as quickly as possible from the station to spend their money in Bahnhofstrasse. While the pedestrian crossing is being built, access by car to the station has been further restricted.

One might have foolishly thought that a pedestrian crossing was a simple matter of putting a bit of paint on the road. But this is a Swiss pedestrian-crossing and requires computer-controlled traffic lights, marble ramps, altering the curbs and moving a lift that serves an underground shopping area. The bill will be in excess of a million francs.

Meeting or dropping off people at the station has become an art. There is nowhere which is neither taxi rank, bus stop nor no-stopping zone. Perhaps people will forget the train altogether and go by car all the way to their destinations.

Although Swiss trains are now more punctual then ever, 80% are less than a minute late and 95% are less than five minutes late. No doubt, soon they will start arriving early. British Rail Southern Region by contrast was forced by the British Advertising Standards Authority to withdraw an advertisement that claimed 89% of their trains were on time. What was wrong with their ad? British Rail classified trains that were up to five minutes late as on time and omitted cancellations from their figures altogether.

How do the Swiss railways do it? Money is mainly the answer – investment in new rolling stock and the latest technology. Add to this a few old-fashioned things like hard work and you have the recipe for a successful rail system. A dirty Swiss train is rarer than a late one. But, like all railways, the Swiss one still makes a thumping loss each year.

JANUARY 19th:

It is now three and a half years since we moved to Zurich and to our present flat. We took it because we had no other choice, but have been extremely lucky nevertheless. Getting a sensibly priced flat in town is virtually impossible. We found our flat through an old friend of Regula. We heard about it before the landlords advertised the flat in the paper. Regula phoned from England and wrote a letter to the owners, the Müller family. They liked her letter and wanted to see us, so we flew out from England for a weekend to make ourselves known to our prospective landlord and landlady. The flat is small, in a quiet road and handy for most things and above all affordable, and we got it.

The flat rental market has eased considerably since we first arrived, but is still difficult. We have had a chance to get to know the area better and have decided we would prefer to live a little out of the town, maybe near the lake. We need more space, we cannot keep expecting guests to sleep on the dining-room floor. Some even do it during dinner. The east coast of the lake is called the 'gold coast' probably for its property prices as much as the fact that it catches the golden evening sun.

The side we fancy is a little less expensive, does not get the evening sun and is called the *Pfnüsel* coast, literally the runny-nose coast. You can provide your own explanation for this.

JANUARY 22nd:

That daft business of inspecting banknotes at supermarket checkouts first spotted in England last year has now reached Switzerland. It happened to a man in front of me in our little local Migros. He was dressed in workmen's clothes and it was a Sfr 1000 (£475) note. After a cursory check, it was accepted for only Sfr 15 worth of groceries and his change was instantly forthcoming from the till without delay.

Not only do the British have no notes larger than £50 (Sfr 110), but even they are difficult to spend as shops do not carry enough cash to give change.

JANUARY 25th:

In an English conversation class we had the following question to discuss; "What sort of work colleague is the worst you can imagine?" We had the usual ideas about humourless, raw-garlic-eating types who do not wash. Then a rather pale and quiet young woman said very sadly, with a deep sigh that comes only from bitter experience: "The worst kind of person to work with is someone who is better at everything than I am!"

A depressing thought for the winter months, but what better than to book an early spring holiday in the Greek Isles? So that is what we have done. A walking holiday on the Greek island of Ikaria, which is near Samos, which is in turn near Patmos, who is the sister of Stirling Moss.

FEBRUARY 2nd:

The flock of the church where Regula's parents go have a problem getting people to do the job of vicar or vicarine (definitely not in the dictionary) and cannot be too choosy. However they have been particularly unlucky with the two ministers sharing the job at the moment.

The first, a man, has a girlfriend with whom he lives and they have had a child together. But the minister cannot marry his girlfriend. Why not? The reason is simple: the minister's wife (and their two children) won't let him!

The second minister is a woman who got herself involved with an asylum-seeker. So close was this involvement that she has given birth to his child. Are they married now, setting a fine example of family life for the parishioners? Are they fiddle! Why not? You guessed it – his wife won't let him. For whilst seeking asylum here, he left behind a wife and goodness knows how many kids. What an odd state of affairs, if that is the right expression.

FEBRUARY 12th:

Regula's Uncle Robert, now in his ninetieth year, is still fairly mobile and he has a season ticket for the classical concert-hall in Zurich. But he has difficulty walking the six minutes from his house to his local railway station. How does he get to the station and not spend all his pension on taxi fares? He hitchhikes! In the nicest possible way. He lives next door to a supermarket and while people are loading up their cars to go home, he asks if he could possibly have a lift round the corner to the station. No one refuses him, even if it is out of their way.

FEBRUARY 25th:

A student said her brother-in-law was a doctor and once had an American patient. The doctor's English was a bit rusty and he could not recall the English for 'pain', so rather slickly he substituted the French word for pain, *douleurs*. This produced the opening sentence: "Good morning, please sit down. Now, where are your *douleurs*?"

The American was taken aback, but realised that all he had heard about the Swiss medical profession was true. He got out his wallet to show the doctor that he had an adequate supply of dollars to meet the bill.

My medical brother-in-law also has an interesting line in English. Andreas has confused for many years the German word *dick* meaning fat, and the English word 'thick', often used to mean stupid. Thus he has been advising bemused and overweight English-speaking patients their problem was that they were simply too thick. But that was polite when compared with what he told his patients to do as he listened to their breathing with his stethoscope. He ordered them to inspire, rather than to breathe in. Then he asked them if they would be so good as to expire for him.

FEBRUARY 28th:

The cost of official Zurich rubbish-bags, which we have to put our rubbish out in, is bound to go up soon because it is cheaper than the previous system. It is surprising how much you can fit in a bag when it costs a lot. We used to use two thirty-five-litre bags a week, now we squeeze it all in one sixteen-litre bag once a week. But that pales against Regula's parents who, in the first eight weeks of the scheme, have used only one thirty-five-litre bag. That one was supplied free-of-charge on the introduction of the system. I think they are filling their cellar with their rubbish.

MARCH 5th:

Two years ago the Swiss PTT (post office) fell into the terrible trap of starting a two-tier postal system. The British did the same thing more than twenty-five years ago with the introduction of first and second class post. It took about twenty years for the British system to be accepted and it looks as though it will take as long for the ripples to settle from the introduction of the Swiss system. Switzerland has no class system so their two-tier postal system is called A and B post. Like the British post office, someone in the Swiss PTT thought it would be a good idea to print a massive 'A' on the A rate stamps. This they did on 80 *Rappen* stamps, which is for domestic A post. Unfortunately it is also the rate for B post to the rest of Europe. So B post now goes to England, for example, with stamps displaying a large A on them.

Confused? Well, remember the Zurich electricity company's campaign to save electricity? Now that the use of electricity is the lowest in forty years, they are putting up the price by 14% to pay for the savings the public has made.

MARCH 12th:

I have a particularly slow class of beginners this term. One lady in the class, who is repeating the first term again, asked me what the English for 'mountain bike' was. So I asked her what the German for 'kindergarten' was – she had no idea.

MARCH 26th:

The Swiss voted 'yes' to a 20% price increase in petrol. The reason they said yes was that, apart from having the cheapest petrol this side of the Rio Grande, the government promised to spend some of the money on the roads – and the poor Swiss voters believed them.

A proposal to stop the ban on *Spielbanken* also received a 'yes'. I did not take much notice until I found out what *Spielbanken* means. They are not 'play banks' or even piggy banks, but casinos. Switzerland plans to become another Monte Carlo in a few years' time, hoping to entice us tourists and bring in more of Switzerland's favourite crop, money.

MARCH 28th:

The Swiss government has realised that smoking is killing their voters – 22% of men and 38% of women in Canton Zurich who die before they are 72, die of cancer. A further 18% and 12% respectively from heart and circulation problems, both of which are smoking related. Only 16% and 9% respectively die of accidents and, surprisingly, 12% of both men and women who die before they are 72, die of suicide. I hope it is not catching.

To cut consumption and raise more money, the Swiss government have put up the price of cigarettes. At the same time as the price increase, a wholesale cartel that controlled the price of tobacco, collapsed. The result is that by buying cigarettes at a supermarket in cartons of 200 the price is now lower than before the government put it up. It makes me want to start smoking again. Cigarettes in Switzerland are half the British price. Like most of Switzerland, the insurance company that Regula works for is confused about smoking. They sell life insurance and at the same time smoking in the offices is rife. They even have a cigarette vending-machine on their premises.

This fits neatly into the weird concept of safety the Swiss have. All houses must be built with a nuclear-proof cellar in which to hide in case the bomb drops. But the only way we can get out of our building is with a key in a very efficient lock. If fire breaks out in the night, we have to fumble our way down the stairs, maybe in thick smoke, making sure that we have our door key with us. However in case of nuclear attack we will be fine.

It is like Swiss parents who make their children wear crash helmets for skiing. Then, at the end of the day, the helmets are tossed in the boot of the car. The kids bounce around the back of the car loose without a seat belt or kiddie-seat as they hurtle home along the autobahn bumper to bumper at 120kph.

MARCH 30th:

We went skiing for the weekend with the sports club of the confused insurance company to Hasliberg. The highlight of the trip was the appearance of a doorman from the insurance company with his blonde girlfriend. She was a Russian thirty years his junior and spoke only a couple of words in German having arrived in Switzerland fourteen days ago. He apparently met her through the Moscow branch of Rent-a-Floozie.

And this is no joke: 44.2% of crime in Canton Zurich is committed by foreigners, while foreigners are only 18.6% of the population. And they say the Swiss are efficient, we foreigners can show 'em!

APRIL 4th:

It must be spring because workmen from the impoverished Zurich council have repainted the garish yellow lines down our road for pedestrians to walk on. These lines are repainted every year, money or no money. The no-waiting signs at the end of our road were starting to look a little dull, they must have been there for at least five years, so they were replaced with shiny new ones.

APRIL 8th:

I have bought a new computer. You did not think I was writing all this by hand, did you? The computer bears the all-important Swiss name, CASH AND CARRY LINE. I am slowly getting used to it, including a Swiss keyboard. The 'z' and 'y' are switched, so I keep writing Yurich instead of Zurich, verz annozing.

We went to the cinema to see the Oscar-winning *Howard's End*. Set in England in about 1910, it is absolutely charming. The acting is good, the scenery, photography and music are excellent, particularly for an English tourist living in Zurich. Not much happens in the film, which is more than can be said for the cinema. The audience felt it necessary to talk and make comments throughout the film. Others crunched popcorn and fidgeted noisily. Then, during the last climatic minutes of the film, the cinema staff flung the doors open to see if the film had finished so they could usher in the next bunch of popcorn-munching giggling punters. It ruined the film for me, and not for the first time. I am seriously considering never going to the cinema again. The cinema has developed into some sort of wider social occasion and we are in the minority in going to watch the film. I certainly cannot be getting old.

APRIL 18th:

Zurich's needle park, having been closed for months, is to reopen after Sfr 1.6 million of the cash-strapped council's money has been spent on cleaning it up. To stop the drug addicts congregating there again, the park will only be open from 11 am to 2 pm for people to have their lunch there. The question is, who in their right mind is going to take their sandwiches there and how much more is it going to cost for the park to be specially opened and closed?

APRIL 19th:

The Monday afternoon Zurich holiday of *Sächsilüüte* (six o'clock ringing) rolled round again. This, like the painting of yellow lines and the digging up of the entire autobahn system always heralds the coming of warmer weather.

You may recall that they burn a snowman as part of this celebration. It is not made of snow but white material that is combustible and its head was stuffed on this occasion with 135 fireworks. The shorter the time taken to blow off the snowman's head the better the summer is supposed to be. On this basis next summer has been cancelled. Ten minutes after the 4.3 metre high (14ft) wood-pile had been lit, the blaze was taking on nicely. Then suddenly the whole bonfire toppled over. The 100 kilo snowman fell off the top before a single flame had reached him. He plunged ignominiously with his arms fixed to his sides, face first into the mud. After consultations, some officials picked up the snowman, but the awkward blighter fell to pieces. They threw his head and some of his bits into the fire. Eventually a few muffled bangs were heard. It was the funniest thing on Swiss TV for many a long year.

APRIL 22nd:

There are no conductors on the Zurich buses and trams. One buys a ticket from a machine or kiosk. Every so often there are flying raids to inspect tickets. It has been more than four months since I had to show my ticket. Because of the forthcoming Easter holidays, my need to use the tram is reduced, and I have not replaced my monthly ticket. I went to school on Monday evening and got a ticket from a machine at the tram stop. The ticket was valid for one hour. Coming back on the tram with some of my students it happened! The tram pulled away from a stop and two burly men in black leather jackets got to their feet and announced that they wanted to see all tickets.

This is a bad enough experience when you have a valid ticket. The driver disables the doors so that no one can escape and you hope that your ticket is OK. I remembered too late that the ticket I had bought on the way there had expired and I was in for a Sfr 50 fine, not to mention the disgrace and humiliation of it all. The inspector asked for my ticket and I told him in broken German my pathetic story of simply forgetting. He shook his head and said it would cost me Sfr 50 and I should get off with him at the next stop to buy a ticket.

Off we got and I went over my whole pitiful tale again. Then, to my amazement, the dark-leather clad storm-trooper relented on the fine, pushed the ticket machine button and indicated that I should now buy a valid ticket. I expressed my relief and thanks, but pointed out as he pushed the button for a twenty-four-hour ticket at Sfr 6, that this should be Sfr 4.60 because of my *Halbtaxabo* (half-fare ticket). I was tempted to ask why it is called a half-fare ticket, when I had to pay more than half price, but thought better of it. No doubt the students on that fateful tram journey wondered if I had been shipped back to Blighty and hoped there would not be any more lessons from me. Well, they are out of luck.

Two weeks in Greece for a well-urned walking holiday. We sent a pile of postcards. However, after seeing how things work out-of-season on the sleepy island of Ikaria, we would not be surprised if the cards never reached their destinations. I have a nasty feeling that the Swiss see the British Isles in much the same light as the British see the Greek Isles – slow, too easy-going and inefficient, but a nice place for a holiday.

The weather was bright and sunny, but a stiff wind kept temperatures down to below 20°C. This was fine for walking, but in the hotel it was chilly at night. There were radiators in our rooms, but they were stone cold. The manager of the hotel, a charming but incorrigible optimist, continually proclaimed with extravagant flourishes of his arms that "tomorrow – zee weather, eet wheel be better!" It never was "better tomorrow."

We eventually convinced the manager that we were much colder than we would be in Switzerland. He hung his head and proffered the excuse that the central-heating pump was broken. Our protests did not abate and, after four nights under double-blankets, he announced that the plumber had paid a visit and the pump was working. The next day it went a degree warmer and the manager turned the heating off again.

Regula's tooth started to trouble her after a couple of days. (I should actually say one of Regula's teeth, as she still has more than one.) She thought it was a root problem and the local dentist confirmed her diagnosis. I thought, judging from the island's inhabitants' general lack of teeth, that he would just whip the tooth out. I was wrong and a series of root treatments was started which involved four visits over the two weeks. The dentist was rather simply equipped and he had no assistant. But Regula, who has extensive experience on the receiving end of dental treatment, said he was excellent. The bill was the equivalent of Sfr 120, which is about a tenth of what it would have cost in Switzerland.

Getting to the dentist was not difficult; we fitted it in at the end of walks and hopped off our old walking-tour bus as it chugged past the end of the dentist's road. The twelve-kilometre journey back to the hotel was less simple, although more interesting. With only half a dozen taxis on the island and no regular bus service, taxis were in great demand. Particularly each time we had finished at the dentist's. We asked the local driving instructor, who was having a snooze in his car between lessons, if he was going our way, and he was. We climbed into the back of his car and he demonstrated that he was descended from a long line of formula-one drivers. He whisked us at breakneck speeds round hairpin bends to his next lesson.

His young customer, introduced to her green-faced passengers as Vicky, was a much slower driver. She took ten minutes to complete the final kilometre and the rest of her lesson to do a twenty-three-point turn in the narrow gravel road outside our hotel. The instructor stubbornly refused to accept any money for the lift and every time he saw us for the rest of our stay on the island he would wave to us and blow his horn loudly as a greeting – at least I think it was a greeting.

That is how things work on the island. Slowly and amicably and without stress or worry. This means that arranging anything Swiss style, where speed and stress are of the essence and friendliness is deemed unnecessary, is an impossibility. We had the middle Sunday free and wanted to hire a motorbike to see some of the island for ourselves. We realised this would be more difficult than just renting one from the establishment outside our hotel that boasted in letters hand-painted by a child on the wall of a concrete hut: "Bikes for Rent".

The optimistic hotel manager explained that this was not his rental business, but that of a friend. With more great flourishes he declared it to be a business with both a licence and insurance. It is considered a novelty to have both. However his friend could not be found, he had lost enthusiasm for the business, as witnessed by the fleet of a dozen rusting Yamahas covered in a winter's grime lying round on the ground. I considered it more likely that we could rent a motorbike in the port, which we could tie in with one of Regula's dental tours. Our walking-guide drove us in the manager's jeep, which I generously filled with petrol costing more than a taxi ride there.

We had to plan ahead because our day off was May 2nd. The day after May 1st, a day (and night) that all Greeks take very seriously. We had been warned that on the evening of May 1st our cold and empty hotel would be transformed into a wild all-night party of feasting and dancing. Fatted animals would be consumed along with vast quantities of wine. Children would be running wild throughout the hotel all night until their parents took them home after a hearty breakfast at eight the following morning. We had been fully briefed and prepared for the worst as earplugs were handed round.

Sadly the band that the manager had booked to play all night did not turn up. That evening he was less cheerful than usual, but at least we got a good night's sleep.

With the-morning-after-the-night-before in mind I thought it better to hire the bike before the celebrations. We arrived in the port to find all the motorbike rental shops boarded up. Our guide kindly offered to phone a number shown on a shop sign. The first one she called was a wrong number, but the second got through to the owner who was rather surprised that anyone should want to rent anything from him and vaguely agreed to come and see us. We took a leisurely coffee at a nearby café and waited.

After ten minutes a young girl arrived and asked if we had phoned about the motorbike. She explained that she was the wrong number, but felt sure that she could find someone to help us. Sure enough, she stopped her young cousin, no older than thirteen years, as he rode past on his motorbike. It was unclear what her cousin's function was, but he had the useful ability to open up the motorbike shop without a key.

Inside, we beheld a sorry sight. Flat-tyred rusting Yamahas again, some without wheels. Not easily beaten, the lad who had opened up the shop said I could rent his bike. The front brake did not work, but he said that did not matter because the back one was very good.

A contract was found, filled in with some difficulty and I was ready to go. They did not want a deposit as there would be no one there to give it back to me when I returned the machine. I was asked to leave the key and the money for the rental with the man who ran the sweet kiosk in the square opposite.

I did not meet the owner of the hire shop until that evening at our hotel where he had come to hear the band that did not turn up. I had to see him as all the petrol had poured out of the motorbike's tank. His answer, in English, to my complaint was very philosophical: "When things are good, they are good and when things are bad, they are bad." He sipped on his Ouzo and boasted that he was a graduate of an English university. He could not recall the name of the university, but confidently told me that he had studied there for over six months. I steered the conversation gently back to the subject of his motorbike. I left him innocently believing that when he said "After I finish my Ouzo, I will fix it," that he would fix it after he had finished his Ouzo.

Next morning, in the cold light of day, the empty-tanked Yamaha stood outside the hotel and another lesson in life was driven, if that is the appropriate verb, surely home. The motorbike had not been touched. Now that the petrol had evaporated, I could see the problem. With a swift snip from my trusty Swiss Army Knife, I removed the end of the fuel pipe with the hole in it. A bit more pipe was tugged through and 'hey presto' all was righted. All, that is, except for the obtaining of fuel on a Sunday when the normally sleepy isle was anaesthetized. The manager, who had regained his optimism after the nonappearance of the musicians, said that the petrol station was open that morning and that our guide could take me there in his jeep. With a plastic one-and-a-half litre Coke bottle in hand, off we went. Needless to say, the garage was closed.

This was annoying as Regula and I had agreed to meet up with a character by the name of Zakaria, who worked behind the bar of the hotel by night and painted the empty swimming pool by day. He promised that his village had caves. Caves with bats and caves without bats. Natural caves and mines for unspecified metals. These were secret and had been used in the war by his villagers to hide from the Italians, and later by the Italians to hide from the British. He gave us directions and we arranged to meet at midday in his village about four kilometres up in the hills. We needed the petrol. Our guide said that she would try at the place where she rented our bus and after a couple of coffees with the proprietors, they filled the Coke bottle with petrol.

After bouncing up a dirt road, Regula and I found the village. We presented ourselves at the village's only shop, which doubled as a café and telephone exchange. It was no more than a room with a door and two windows. Zakaria, our intrepid cave guide, was still asleep. His kind white-haired old mother who ran the café, hobbled next door with her walking stick to wake him.

Once he had been invigorated by a late breakfast of herb tea with bread stuffed in it, we were ready to go. Me with Regula clinging on the pillion and Zakaria with the local Greek Orthodox priest on the back of his motorcycle. Regula and I had a debate as to whether he was the local priest. He was introduced to us as Janis, or John. When I asked what relation he was to Zakaria, there was laughter and we were informed that he was the *Papa*, which we later learned means father or the priest. We have our doubts, he was a chain smoker for a start.

After fifteen minutes bumping up a dusty trail and a couple of stops for arguments between our guide and the priest, we reached an overgrown field. We made our way through rough bush to a small hollow. This was no more than an indentation with a bit of water in it. To one edge there was what looked to us like a fox hole. Proudly Zakaria announced that this was the entrance to the famous Cave of Mandria. We smiled and thanked him and thought that would be the end. But no, we were expected to take photographs of the expedition. After the photo-session, Zakaria, the only man on the island with a crash helmet, put it on and indicated that he was about to enter the cave with his trusty pocket torch.

After five minutes of struggling and wiggling and a few false starts, he lay prone on the ground with nothing more than his Wellington boots visible. The priest had meanwhile smoked three more cigarettes. Zakaria extracted himself, his clothes stained with mud, to report that the cave went on for at least thirty metres and then turned off to the right, whilst indicating left with his hand. He invited me to inspect the wonders of Mandria for myself, but I declined the tempting offer. It will be some years before the Cave of Mandria is on the list of essential tourist attractions on the island.

We were then told we must now see the famous Mine of Mandria. On our way we stopped at a small farm house, the home of Janis the improbable priest. We met his wife who had a small beard and was, like most of the islanders, in urgent need of dental treatment. Through the course of the afternoon we were fed the best food we had on the holiday. They produced everything themselves – cheese, pork in lemon jelly, goat meat, olives, potatoes, salad, bread and plenty of wine.

We survived the afternoon's festivities without any ill effects and were able to confirm that it will also be some years before the Mine of Mandria becomes a tourist must. I could at least enter the mine, but not stand up straight and, like our holiday, it ended very soon after it started.

MAY 10th:

Our car battery was flat when we got back. But the shock of starting teaching again was blunted by one student who, when asked what the opposite of 'married' was, brightly replied that it must be 'happy'!

Regula and I had lunch and ostrich steak was on the menu. Always willing to try something new, we ordered a couple. It was more like rump steak than chicken, and quite forgettable. But Regula did run back to her office faster than usual.

Speaking of meat, Regula noticed a little article in the paper saying that Swiss consumption of pork was dropping (or was it dripping?) Lamb these days was rare. And best of all, horse meat remained stable.

MAY 17th:

We've found a flat! It is just outside the city limits of Zurich on the west side of the lake where the trains and noses run. The flat has two balconies, to make up for having no balcony at our present one. It has extensive views over the lake and, when the weather is clear, of the snow-capped mountains. There is a bus stop at the end of the road and the journey takes just eight minutes to the front door of Regula's office. The same bus gets me to school in ten minutes.

I'm sure that moving will be a complicated matter, what with registering and de-registering with the local community offices. The hardest part will be telling our present landlords, the Müllers, as we have got on so well with them.

Theoretically we should give three months' notice to move in either April or October, but it is accepted that this does not work in practice. As long as we find one suitable tenant to replace us, there is no problem. Tenants are easy to find, it is flats that are difficult.

MAY 23rd:

The first item on the Swiss radio news this morning was not about a war or famine, but the new rail timetable which came into force today. Swiss life

seems dominated by railways and the Swiss know how to run them. We went to Berne last week and the fastest train there is an Inter-European express which starts its journey in Munich. Amazingly it was running twenty minutes late. Did the passengers anxiously waiting at Zurich have to put up with this delay? Of course not. Ten minutes before the scheduled departure time an extra train arrived to take us. This left Zurich and arrived in Berne bang on time. Will the privatised British Rail do such things? One guess and no prize.

MAY 24th:

We move at the end of next month and to find a suitable tenant to replace us, we have put a three line classified advertisement under a box number in the newspaper. Regula has also put a card on the notice board at her office.

MAY 27th:

Regula has already arranged for five different parties from her work to view the flat! After we had shown the first couple round the flat, the postman staggered to our letter box with seventy replies to the ad in the paper. Amazing replies they were too. Two applicants included a photocopy from their local court confirming they did not have any debts and had never been sued for nonpayment of bills. One man even advised us what his salary was. It was like looking into people's private lives. We handed the letters over to the Müllers with the idea that, if they discounted the poor quality photocopied replies, ones with spelling mistakes and took only those who are non-smokers without pets or children and included a stamped addressed envelope, they should still have more than half a dozen to choose from.

The experience made me wonder how on earth we managed to get our new flat, which was also through an ad in the paper under a box number and even more how we got the first flat writing from England. Regula has the answer, she says it is because we are non-smokers without pets or children and she writes such good letters.

JUNE 1st:

We are starting to pack things into boxes for our move. The colonial history of England is reflected in the fact that the British pack things in tea chests when they move. I am not quite sure what it says about Switzerland, but here we pack things in banana boxes.

JUNE 4th:

The legal side of moving is much simpler in Switzerland than in the UK because there are no lawyers or estate agents involved. Moving can also be a lot quicker: we have heard of people who have moved within a week of finding a flat they liked. It is such a 'landlords' market', that people have to take what they want quickly. The British reckon on three months or more for moving.

Swiss rental rules state that we have to leave the flat as we found it. All the holes made to hang up pictures have to be filled, the walls have to be washed down and the floors and carpets cleaned. Had we been extravagant and painted the walls, then we would have to repaint them in the original colour.

We are going to pay a company to do the cleaning and, after our back-breaking experience with 'Van Hire and Friend', we are hiring a removal company. What we save on lawyers and estate agents, we spend on cleaners and movers.

JUNE 7th:

Regula has decided that it is time to change her *Heimatort* (home town) from the hamlet of Aeschi in Canton Solothurn back to the town of Zurich, which was her previous *Heimatort*. It would be bad enough to fall on hard times, without having to up and move to another canton. The town president (or mayor) has to give his approval to such matters. Regula has been thrown into top gear – rushing from police station to community office collecting assorted pieces of paper saying how wonderful she is, each piece costs at least Sfr 15. Then the people of Zurich want Sfr 350 to let her join them.

JUNE 10th:

The Swiss take all the light fittings when they move and leave just bare wires. Very un-British, where a light fitting and bulb is always left in each room so that the new occupants can see something of their new home after dark on the first evening.

We received a post card from my mother and father on holiday in Canada. Mum is the writer and she is famous for her eccentric handwriting. The card was written from the CN Tower in Toronto – they must have the *Föhn* in Canada too, because she writes that on a clear day one can see Nigeria from up there.

JUNE 15th:

In the rule book of Regula's confused insurance company it states that she is entitled to "one to two days' holiday" for moving, so like everyone else who moves, she is going to take two days off. It is the same amount off she would get if I died. Their priorities are confused too.

JUNE 28th:

The Swiss people have just voted 'no' to an initiative that would have stopped a Swiss government plan to buy thirty-four American jet fighter planes at a cost of untold billions of francs. In other words they can buy them after all. So our walks in the mountains should be noisier in the future as the Swiss air force play with their new toys.

JULY 4th:

After a whirlwind of packing, new address notifying, community office visiting, we moved. Our moving day, July 1st, was just three days short of our fourth anniversary in Switzerland. It did not rain and the move went painlessly. Four years ago the police reserved a parking space for the van at a cost of Sfr 35. This time I made a couple of signs out of cardboard and hung them on the fence to ward off parkers on the day we moved. Regula had misgivings about her countrymen's ability to follow such unofficial directions written on a home-made sign in felt-tipped pen. She was wrong – it worked a treat.

We made two big mistakes when we moved from England to Switzer-land. Firstly we moved from a moderate house and tried to put our quart of belongings in a pint pot of a flat. Secondly I wasted a lot of time working out beforehand what should go in what room. The result was that after we had finished unloading, every room was filled with a heap of boxes and furniture. This blocked our progress and each box we opened to let its contents escape exasperated the situation. This time around I wised up and, other than beds and chairs, everything else went into one room. This left the other rooms relatively empty and gave a dangerous illusion that we had some sort of order in the new flat long before we had.

The new flat is living up to our expectations and the constantly changing view across the lake is wonderful. It is surprising how many police wearing sunglasses patrol the lake in speed boats – now that's a good job. We are a matter of metres outside Zurich's city-limits and already we are in the country. People say *Grüetzi* to me as I walk down the road. (Here it means 'hello, old boy'.) Far from making me feel as though I have been living in Switzerland for four years, moving to the lake shore has made me feel even more like a tourist.

JULY 8th:

More 'T-shirt English' seen today. A young woman student came to one of my classes with an expensive T-shirt delicately embroidered with a heart and the lyrics immortalised by the American harmony group of the 50s, the Platters, "O M L Y Y O U !" I said it was very nice, omly next time perhaps she should take her English dictionary with her when she goes shopping.

JULY 13th:

We had to de-register with the town hall in Zurich when we left and prove that we were up to date with our tax payments, then register with the new community office when we arrived. That part, believe it not, was free of charge, as were the address changes in our driving licences. Then my papers arrived and, after paying Sfr 54, I can stay and work here for another year. The papers have been checked by the *Fremdenpolizei*. I used to think that this meant 'thought police', but now I know a little more German I can see that it means 'stranger police'. My only question now is: stranger than what?

Somehow we have both lost a couple of kilos in weight and it was completely unplanned. We are unclear how this has been achieved. It could be that the last few weeks of running around preparing for and then making the move has done it. I refurbished the bathroom scales after the move and they look much better now, but are they accurate? I need a second opinion.

Life goes on as ever: the man from the *Bahnhof Buffet* is just back from his customary jaunt to the exotic side of life. This time he was island hopping in the Seychelles.

JULY 16th – AUGUST 1st:

No sooner have we moved than we hop off to England. I booked the tickets long ago, before we knew we would move, so we are wrenched from unpacking to the vagaries of a British summer, which I am pleased to report was cold, wet and windy. Our schedule there became more gruelling with each day that passed, as we tried to visit as many people as possible. I paid my usual visit to the dentist. No, I do not cheat and have it done free on the British National Health system. My dentist left 'The Health' five years ago. I pay a private insurance in the UK – about £10 (Sfr 22) per month. It means that it is cheaper to buy a plane ticket to England and visit the dentist than have my teeth done at Swiss prices. Switzerland must have the most expensive dental treatment in the world, but contrary to the law of supply and demand, the Swiss appear from their symmetrical smiles to visit their dentists more than the British.

Strangely we met up with our former landlords, the Müller family, while in England. They rented a cottage in the Cotswolds for their summer holidays. Because of heavy traffic, it took them over four hours to drive the two-hour journey to the south coast to see us. When we eventually met up we were able to show them a number of notable local traffic queues.

A few years ago Margaret Thatcher made an ill-advised statement to the effect that Britain lead the rest of Europe in environmental matters. If there is a shred of truth in her statement, then I have seen no evidence of it. 'Bottle banks' exist for recycling glass, but otherwise there is none of the recycling paraphernalia so familiar to those who live in Switzerland – separate collection for aluminium or other metals and regular collection of newspapers and cardboard. Deposit bottles went out in the 1960s in Britain where dead batteries, newspapers and potato peel still go out the same way – into the dustbin.

Our final Sunday in England was August 1st, Swiss National Day. We celebrated with the Bournemouth Swiss club at a cool and windy barbecue in the New Forest. When we lived in England we helped run this club which has the ingenious name of 'The Wilhelm Tell Group'. Of the forty Swiss with British partners, two are Swiss men and the remaining Swiss, as you might expect, are women. Most went over to England as teenagers to learn English, were waylaid by Englishmen and settled down there. Despite, or perhaps because they are living in England and not Switzerland, they declare that they prefer to live in England. Confident predictions were made before we left four years ago that we would be back within months. Many from this Anglo-Swiss group are surprised that we actually like living in Switzerland.

AUGUST 2nd:

Back to Switzerland and wonderful weather. The flight back was fine, once having conquered the morning traffic on the M25 motorway round London. To try and alleviate congestion, the M25 is to be widened to fourteen lanes. I cannot see that it will be worthwhile and what will the environmental cost be? Just a minute, I'm not starting to sound Swiss am I?

After sweltering from the airport to our local railway station in the unfamiliar heat of the Swiss summer, I left Regula with the cases and went to get the car. As I walked up the hill, I noticed more and more cars with flat tyres. It was clear that the tyres had been slashed, or to be more accurate, stabbed. Sadly our car was a victim too. Someone had celebrated August 1st by destroying the tyres of twenty-five cars down our road and a further twenty-five within the city limits of Zurich. This I learned later from our local police officer (at least I think he was a police officer, he was dressed in jeans and a T-shirt). He was most apologetic when I went to his office to get a form to try to claim the tyres off our insurance. It was as if it were his fault – perhaps it was.

While I removed the two wheels with punctured tyres... ah ha, you wonder, how is that possible with only one spare tyre? Don't forget that every good Swiss, and this good tourist, has a set of winter wheels that spend their summers in the cellar. I simply put two of the winter wheels on. While I did this hot and dirty job, I was constantly interrupted by neighbours driving past and stopping to ask if I too had been a victim of the tyre stabber. I was able to find out the best place locally for new tyres. But, after having the cheapest Polish-made remoulds I could find fitted, the good old confused insurance company agreed to repay the cost completely. I should have had low profile racing tyres fitted to the right-hand side of the car.

AUGUST 5th:

The Swiss government are having another attempt at getting to grips with the drug problem. Whether drug taking is any worse in Switzerland than other countries is unclear. It is like AIDS, in that the Swiss are probably one of the few nations in the world that actually has a good idea of how many of its inhabitants are infected. The result is that Switzerland appears to have an above average occurrence of AIDS and HIV infection. So it is with drugs.

In an otherwise ordered land, Switzerland's drug problem stands out like a sore thumb and attracts much adverse publicity. The problem afflicts all large towns and in Zurich is limited to about 900 known addicts. The national government has decided to open centres to dish out drugs at Sfr 10 per day to some of these registered addicts. The Swiss want to control every facet of their lives and the consumption of drugs is no different. By dispensing drugs below 'street' prices, the trade in drugs should be severely cut. I fear that, like the free-needle policy, cheap drugs on the state will only make matters worse, but I would like to be proved wrong.

With a strong will, the drug problem could be dealt with in days. The resources are there, but the will seems lacking. The Swiss have shown in environmental matters that, with enough political will, anything is possible. Swiss dog owners have been persuaded to pick up their dogs' 'do' in public places and put it into special green 'doggie-do' containers. (These containers have a Swinglish name: *Robidog*.) It surely proves that if you can get dog owners to do this, then anything is possible.

While the national government was deciding to hand out hard drugs, the government of the Canton of Zurich decided that anyone wishing to purchase more than 50 Aspirins in one go, must in future have a prescription from their doctor. Not to be outdone, the red/green Zurich town council have suggested that newspaper dispensers in the streets should no longer be in the red or blue of the papers' choice, but should be painted grey. The local press had a field day with this. The Zurich weekly newspaper, called with cunning logic *Züri Woche* (Zurich Week), usually has a blue banner and colour pictures, came out with a special grey edition. This included pictures of grey trams, grey post boxes and grey policemen – the rest of the town is already grey.

However, the Zurich town council are not quite as daft as they may at first appear, as they earned a tidy Sfr 4 million from speeding motorists caught in the iron gaze of their force of metal policemen. (The automatic camera and flash boxes that caught me so unfairly once.) There are only five cameras in use in the town, which are moved round the dozens of boxes. The presence of these boxes alone is a great deterrent to would-be speedsters. You can usually spot where these metal policemen are positioned by the black skid-marks in the road.

AUGUST 12th:

A mastermind from the Swiss criminal underworld has started forging five franc coins. The coin is a big solid affair and an odd thing to forge. It must cost a lot in metal alone. I could not see why anyone should want to do it. But I had forgotten that the Swiss are great collectors – from the foil tops of coffee creamers, to metal lapel badges (*Pins* in Swinglish). These forged coins have become very collectable, so collectable that the police have managed to lay their hands on only one example. The others are changing hands at some Sfr 30 a piece. Supermarket checkout-girls now check Sfr 1000 notes to see if they are genuine and Sfr 5 coins in the hope that they are not.

AUGUST 14th:

When we were over in England, I drove much more than I have for a long while. The result is that now I keep trying to get into the front passenger's door instead of the driver's door. It is a habit that I thought I had got rid of long ago. Half a dozen times since we got back from England I have found myself opening the passenger's door with keys in hand ready to drive off. It is very embarrassing and I have to pretend to be looking for something before assuming the driver's side.

AUGUST 17th:

Our new landlady is away on a walking holiday on the Isle of Man of all places. I took her to the railway station so that she could send her case all the way to Douglas, the island's main town, by the great Swiss 'Fly Baggage' system. You wave goodbye to your cases at your local railway station and meet them again at your destination airport. It sounds very dangerous, but it works. The man at the local station had never heard of the Isle of Man. He asked if it was not the Isle of Wight she wanted. I must say, I had the same thought myself when she told me where she was going.

A graffiti whiz-kid has sprayed the following on the local railway station wall: "*Schlule, nein danke!*", when translated it would be something like: "Skool, no thanks!" Which rather speaks for itself. The same dyslexic sprayer also had a go in English with "**** the sistem". Another sprayer in a different colour has since corrected his spelling of system.

This reminds me of some American graffiti that read "I love grils." Then somebody changed grils to girls. However a further sprayer added, "Hey, what about us grils?!?"

AUGUST 20th:

I reported that moving had meant we both had lost a little weight. That now needs correcting and it is all because of clouds. Regula and I were sitting with her parents in their garden looking at what faces we could spot in the gathering thunder clouds. (Her parents don't have cable television.) Her father spotted Mickey Mouse and jumped up to point it out to us. He walked backwards and looked up at the same time, lost his balance and disappeared into the shrubbery. Unfortunately he caught his forehead on a stone which bled rather a lot (his head, not the stone). We had to rush him off to Doc Andreas', who was luckily still at his practice late in the evening doing some long-overdue paperwork by the light of his X-ray viewer (yes really). Regula's father needed two stitches in his forehead, which were actually metal staples from a little machine that looked awfully like a common-or-garden paper stapler.

While we were waiting for Regula's father to be stapled back together, we took turns in playing with the various medical gadgets that were lying around. We weighed ourselves and were shocked to find that we were no longer our new slimmer selves. We protested that the scales were wrong, but everyone else weighed themselves and declared them to be accurate. We sadly have to admit that, rather than us losing weight in the move, our scales seem to have somehow been knocked out of skew, probably when I cleaned them up.

SEPTEMBER 10th:

The Isle of Man was a big hit with our new landlady. Anywhere that is different from Switzerland holds a great attraction for the Swiss. So a small island with a miserable climate, lashed by cold westerly gales and salty sea spray, with a cuisine that depends heavily on potatoes cooked in fat and vegetables boiled to death, where the sheep and cows have no bells, is just up their street.

SEPTEMBER 17th:

Swiss school classes, particularly at younger levels, stay with the same teacher for three years or more and the teacher takes nearly all subjects, whereas the British system has a different teacher for each subject, usually only for one year. The Swiss system tends to bind the class and the teacher together (or force them apart as the case may be).

The result is that class reunions are a common feature of Swiss life. They may not occur every year but they seem to go on until all the class has died off. Regula's class of 1960 to 1963 are all alive and kicking and are to get together for the weekend in a few weeks' time in the Bernese Oberland where their teacher now lives. Regula's father had a class reunion a few weeks ago. His reunion is remarkable for the fact that this time his teacher could not be with them, but he sent a note saying that he hoped to be with them again next time. The teacher is ninety-three years old. Maybe teaching is going to be good for me in ways I had not previously considered.

Regula's mother attended her class reunion a couple of years ago. She had not seen the class for many years. When she entered the private room at the restaurant reserved for them, she thought she must have got the wrong place as it was full of elderly white-haired men and women.

SEPTEMBER 24th:

Another teaser: how many circuses are there in Switzerland? While you are thinking, let me tell you about my new computer. It suddenly stopped and I could not restart it. Thinking I had been sold a pup, I rushed back to the shop where I bought it. They detected a virus that had destroyed everything that I had ever written on the computer. How did my computer get a virus? In my enthusiasm for my new computer's gallons of empty hard-disc space, I gratefully accepted offers of free games. This seems the most likely source. Fortunately I had backed up everything onto floppy discs and lost nothing. When I got my computer back, I was wiser, a few hundred francs poorer, but still in possession of everything that I had ever written on it, like the following paragraph.

Switzerland's roads are blighted with holes, kindly dug by guest workers. These holes do not seem to serve much purpose and soon after they have been dug they are filled again, unless of course the hole is somewhere very inconvenient, in which case it can remain open for months.

Swiss holes-in-the-road are very different from British ones. British holes are surrounded by mounds of assorted earth and rock, which was under the ground before it was a hole. Swiss holes, by stark contrast, are moundless. Their sides are straight and the edges swept and earthless. This has troubled me for a long time, until the other day when I spotted a hole being made. The earth is flung onto a lorry. The lorry is then driven off, probably to fill in another hole somewhere else in a road nearby. Because there are so many holes being dug and filled, within a few years Switzerland's entire subsoil to a depth of two metres will have been swopped around and mixed together. This is going to cause pandemonium among archaeologists for centuries to come.

The number of circuses in Switzerland is twenty-nine. All in the circus game agree it is far too many, but they just cannot help it. Put half a dozen Swiss together and they go out and buy a tent and start taming lions and pouring water down their trousers.

Speaking of circuses; our begging letter situation is now out of control. We asked for our mail to be forwarded from our old address for one year. At Sfr 5 this has to be the biggest bargain in Switzerland. We gave up trying to stop these begging letters a long time ago. We have sent them back with stamps marked "not required". We have sent them back without stamps. We have thrown them away unopened, but they still keep on coming. Since moving, we get the ones for our old address plus a whole new range of begging letters directed to our new address.

OCTOBER 1st:

The Swiss criminal mastermind who forged five franc pieces is a genius. His forgeries are becoming more and more sought after and their market value has risen to Sfr 150. Now more five franc fiddles have come to light.

Some tourist hot-foot back from Moscow discovered that a Russian rouble coin is exactly the same size as the solid Swiss five franc piece. Are these roubles being collected too?

Not exactly, the Zurich public transport system has altered their ticket machines to stop collecting roubles instead of five franc pieces. But not before they had lost Sfr 125,000. Which I estimate must mean they collected a cool 25,000 Rouble coins.

The Swiss hunting season will be under way again shortly. They shoot deer, chamois, ibex and the occasional tourist. It is tightly controlled and a licence will set you back Sfr 600 if you are Swiss or live in Switzerland. If you are a tourist then be prepared to fork out Sfr 12,000. And still there is no guarantee that you will shoot anything.

OCTOBER 13th:

We bought a telescope to make full use of our new view. We have looked through it so much that we are in danger of wearing it out. Yesterday evening we had a Scandinavian couple over, he is Swedish and she is Finnish, for a smorgasbord. We did not really eat that, but it reminds me of an odd advertisement in the trams for Zurich's central-station-and-building-site buffet. The advertisement was on a small card with words so huge that only four letters would fit per line. It took me months to realise that *S'MOR GAS BORD* didn't mean that some more gas board was obtainable at the buffet, but the traditional Norse table of pickled fish and stale bread.

Meanwhile back at the telescope. We took turns looking for the Scandinavian couple's flat on the other side of the lake. We soon found it, but discovered one of them had left a light on. With disgruntled looks, he said it was the Finn, and she said it was the Swede.

OCTOBER 19th:

An interesting aspect of teaching adults is the diverse occupations students have. A fellow teacher has the second violinist from the Zurich concert orchestra in one of her classes. I suggested that in learning English he is trying to add another string to his bow. Either that or he is tired of playing second fiddle.

OCTOBER 25th:

Swiss motorists are notorious for not stopping for pedestrians, even on pedestrian crossings. Last week a man jumped out onto a crossing in front of a car. The car was able to stop, but the one behind did not and ran into the back of the one that did. The court decided that it was the pedestrian's fault and he was fined. What I cannot understand is why the pedestrian was daft enough to hang around after he had caused the accident and have his name taken – I always run away as fast as I can.

OCTOBER 30th:

We have the choice of three modes of public transport near our flat. The bus is the one we use the most. Bus drivers attend the same training course as the tram drivers where they are taught that the timetable is king and passengers come second. The buses belt along their routes, waiting for nobody and flinging from side to side the lucky few who managed to get on. The transport company call their passengers rather sweetly, *Fahrgäste*, which means 'travel guests'. This is a classic Swiss euphemism, as guests are not usually expected to pay.

We can also take the train, a new double-decker *S-Bahn* (fast train), nicknamed the 'Lambada Express' after the song and dance popular when the train was introduced. The Lambada involved couples cavorting in very close proximity to one another. The seats are so close in the new train that much the same effect is supposed to happen to facing passengers. Let me save you a wasted journey – it doesn't.

These trains have guards. I know most trains have guards, but these are additional guards to the guard. In response to those who would like to do the Lambada, or worse, with complete strangers, the carriages are patrolled by uniformed guards with big black boots. Curiously the guards are very concerned about passengers who put their feet up on the seats, but never want to see any tickets. It is assumed that whatever frightful outrage one attempts on Swiss trains, naturally one will have first purchased a valid ticket, guest or no guest.

The third way we can travel is by boat. This is covered with the same ticket as the bus and train. It is by far the most pleasant way to travel, cruising along the lake with other tourists. Some boats have a restaurant and bar so the trip is always in danger of turning into a holiday. The timetable is infrequent and slow, but whoever heard of a tourist in a hurry?

NOVEMBER 6th:

In the USA we found that although the motels had loads of TV channels, every room was tuned to different channel numbers. If we wanted to watch, say channel nine, we had a very frustrating time trying to find it, because channel nine was on any channel but the one numbered nine. Now I understand how this confusion can happen. Our Swiss cable TV operator, REDIFFUSION, is busy recabling the canton. This is so we can have the wonder of thirty-six TV channels. For some reason the cable company have changed some channels they send their signals on. We woke up this morning to find CNN is now where France 3 was, and France 3 is where CNN was and two other stations were swopped. Worse still, after I had spent the best part of half an hour swopping the channels back to their original numbers on our TV and video, Regula read on the Teletext that viewers shouldn't change the channels, since they would be swopped back again soon. The name of our cable company should be changed too, to Reconfusion.

NOVEMBER 12th:

It is very cold, and my car battery is feeling the strain. I offered to run Regula down to her office. As always we had only moments to spare and discovered too late the battery was flat. Regula leapt out of the car and belted off for the bus. She had only gone a few metres when an elderly lady motorist pulled up and very kindly offered Regula a lift. She was driven to her office door. A neighbourly area this.

The Swiss are to vote for the fourth time on whether they would like to pay value added tax (VAT). It seems like a daft question to me. The proposed rates are 6.2% or 6.7%. How can either rate be added to, for example, a bus ticket costing Sfr 3.80? The British had similar difficulties with 8% VAT so Mrs Thatcher kindly made it 10% so we could work it out more easily. Once we got the hang of that, she tried us on 12.5%. We could do that too, so she tested us with 15% VAT. Mrs T had to go and write her memoirs and John Major came along and the first thing he wanted to know was if we could handle 17.5% VAT. It was a breeze. The British public are now eagerly awaiting the challenge of VAT at 20%, then 22.5%, then 25%...

NOVEMBER 21st:

The everyday Swiss are still going to exotic parts for their hols. The Trans-Siberian Railway from Moscow to Peking and a month in the jungles of Ecuador, to name but two examples from students. Whether they enjoy these holidays is another matter. Like a middle-aged woman student who went to Japan and came back three kilos lighter. The reason was, like many Swiss, she did not like raw fish.

NOVEMBER 28th:

As our duvets were showing signs of wear, Regula phoned a company that cleans and revitalises duvets. We cannot spend a duvetless night so the feather-freshening company said they could shake up our down within an hour. With two duvets in the car, off we went.

If Walt Disney had built a factory, this would have been it. Inside the clean, spacious carpeted plant were a lot of strange machines. Through large windows we could see inside the machines where feathers were being blown and tossed about. Each machine was manned by operators in white coats with feathers in their hair. Every one of them said *Grüetzi* to us, shook our hands vigorously and introduced themselves and waited for us to give our surname. After half a dozen feathery introductions, we eventually met the man who was going to fix our duvets. After we had Grüetzied him and shaken hands and exchanged names, he explained that they would suck the feathers out with a big tube, then toss them around in one of their machines for a while. Then the outer covers would be replaced with sleek new ones and filled with our laundered feathers.

We made our way back to the door, shaking hands again and saying goodbye as we went. An hour later we were back. This time we marched purposefully in with hands firmly in our pockets to avoid as many handshakes as possible. We were shown our new duvets, which we hope were filled with our clean feathers and not someone else's. From now on we will be sleeping under recycled duvets.

DECEMBER 8th:

The arguments for adopting VAT obviously appealed to the Swiss nature. Very roughly translated they went like this: *We've gone and spent all your taxes, and a fair bit more. We're up a gum tree and no mistake. But we've some ideas. Try these for size:*

1) VAT at 6.2%, this won't help too much, but it will at least line us up with the rest of Europe, although it's not done them much good.

2) VAT at 6.7%, this should start to clear the mess up, but just in case it doesn't we've come up with option three.

3) VAT at 6.7%, but we can raise it to 7.5% if it's not enough for what we have in mind.

For the life of me, I don't know why, but the Swiss voted in option three. And that is how the curse of western society was to be hoisted on the Swiss.

The voters of Switzerland were also asked if they would like to ban all advertising of tobacco and alcohol. They put down their wine glasses, coughed, stubbed out their cigarettes and gave a firm *nein*.

There was also a vote to approve the Sunday opening of shops in the Canton of Zurich. Sunday opening has been a big issue in the UK for years where the large stores want to open on Sundays because they make more money. The public do not have more to spend, they simply spend less with small shops that do not or cannot open on Sundays. Mr Major should have asked the British public what they think. They gave it a firm *nein* in the Canton of Zurich, although they did agree to a slight extension of shop hours to 8 pm, if the shops want. Shops must still close at 4 pm on Saturdays, which I think is wonderful. If I had a choice, the shops would shut at about midday on weekdays and close the whole weekend – anything to keep me from being dragged round them.

DECEMBER 16th:

One reason why the Swiss smoke so much could be that it's good for the economy, or at least not so bad for it. 80% of the tobacco products sold in Switzerland are made from Swiss-grown tobacco!

DECEMBER 20th:

In Britain as one starts to get a little older, the first thing one notices is that the police seem to look younger. (Then doctors, then lawyers and finally retired people.) I once saw a cartoon of two British bobbies. One said to the other: *"You can tell you're a policeman when the public start to look older."* As the Swiss get older they start to dwell more and more on the pages of the newspaper known as the *Todesanzeigen*, or death announcements.

One's attitude to life can be influenced by what appears in these pages. For example, an insurance executive I know always checks the ages of those who have died, to see if his company is paying out too generously on life insurance policies. Others with an interest in meteorology point out that the number of pages devoted to the *Todesanzeigen* always increases just after a severe blow of Switzerland's natural hair drier and euthanasic wind, the *Föhn*.

This morbid interest seems to be awakened after one reaches forty. But you are not really into studying the stiff-pages until you start reading them first when you pick up the paper. By that time one should see names that you know appearing quite frequently. The *Todesanzeigen* would also help the Swiss update their Christmas-card list, if they had any.

By contrast with Switzerland, Britain goes barmy with cards at Christmas, not only sending them to every distant relative and obscure friend, but handing cards to people they see every day. At this time of year British office workers can be seen taking bundles of cards to work to hand out to their colleagues. They then sit with their desks covered in Christmas cards from people they see every day in their office, even from the person who sits opposite them.

I used to think this was a normal state of affairs, but each time I explain it to my students as part of the British Christmas, it seems more and more ridiculous. I must be slipping.

DECEMBER 25th:

After forty-four years of dreaming of one, it finally came on the forty-fifth. (White Christmas).

DECEMBER 31st:

Another year passes. The optimistic British are still telling themselves that things are getting better, without a shred of evidence. The Swiss are becoming a little numbed to unheard of levels of unemployment, but they are still worrying.

The man from the Bahnhof Buffet, who amazed me with his extravagant holiday destinations and last summer went island hopping in the Seychelles has been 'rationalised'. This sadly means in plain English that he is helping to push up those unemployment figures. At least tourism is still booming.

JANUARY 1st:

We spent New Year with Regula's brother and sister, Andreas and Vroni, and their respective families at Andreas's mountain hut. It was enjoyable and unconventional as usual (the house and the company). The weather was not so kind. Plenty of snow for a change, but it kept on falling while we were there.

Now that we live near the railway and use the train a bit more, I have discovered a very disturbing trick the Swiss railways do to help speed things along. The busy stretch below our flat has only two lines. This, you might expect, is one line 'up' and one 'down'. For most of the time it is, but when things get busy slow trains are passed by expresses using both lines in the same direction. It can be rather unnerving to see an intercontinental express hurtling down the line that not more than a few minutes before bore a train going in the opposite direction. I'm sure they know what they're doing.

JANUARY 6th:

It's clear I am spending far too much time in the *Bahnhof Buffet*. I still go there to eat between lessons at St Addanuf. Not only did they give me a Christmas present, a bag of highly-prized *Bahnhof Buffet* coffee beans, but my first visit in the new year earned me a vigorous handshake from the new manager. He was probably hoping that he won't be rationalised too. The next accolade in the Swiss hierarchy of eating places is a chair with my name on it (scratched into the Formica, no doubt).

JANUARY 12th:

I stumbled across some more T-shirt English today – this time on a scarf in a shop window embroidered with the words "Nobody's Perfekt." Quite so.

Regula's insurance company, like most respectable Swiss companies, is continually having its premises refurbished. When I went past there today, I noticed they were having their central courtyard dug up by a company specialising in boring holes.

In an attempt to be as fashionable as one can in the hole-digging business, this company trades under the Swinglish name of *Swissboring*. It would be even better with an exclamation mark, or question mark, after the name.

JANUARY 14th:

With falling interest rates it has been rumoured that Swiss flat rents should go down. They were increased, sometimes dramatically, over the last three years because of rising interest rates, one of the few grounds for landlords to increase rents. However, like most prices, what goes up hardly ever comes down. We are some of the lucky ones and from April have a rent reduction. That's the good news. The bad news is that the reduction is only 0.2%.

JANUARY 17th:

My sister in England, Angie, has done something very admirable over the last five years. When her two daughters left school, she retired from being a housewife and mother and started studying law. Now she is a fully-qualified solicitor. She loves the work, which is helped by having a continuous stream of oddballs for clients. Like a young lady who, thanks to the British legal-aid system, can visit my sister on a daily basis for legal advice, a cup of tea and a chat. On her first visit this young lady said "I've got a fantastic memory, I never forget anything. Oh, have I told you that before?"

FEBRUARY 3rd:

How much do you think a driving lesson costs in the Zurich area? The standard rate is Sfr 84 for a fifty-minute lesson. That's just over £38. When I learned to drive it was thirty shillings for a full hour or £1.50, a ridiculous Sfr 3.30. I had to put up with a well-used Ford Cortina with plastic seats, rubber floor-mats and plenty of external evidence of previous pupils' errors. Zurich's learners get to stall and kangaroo around town in the latest model BMW or Mercedes.

The police in the Canton of Zurich are never short of a campaign to clobber motorists and have now come up with a purge against 'igloo drivers'. Nothing to do with Pingu the popular penguin TV-series which is made in Switzerland, but motorists who do not clear the frost off their cars before driving in the early morning. Thus it looks as though they are driving an igloo. One hapless motorist went through a metal policeman (speed camera) at 58kph in a 50 zone. This would normally attract a fine of Sfr 20, but as he was driving with frost-covered windows and only a little patch of windscreen cleared in front of his face, he was stung with a Sfr 600 (£273) fine. The weather has not helped the police with their campaign as January was the third mildest one this century.

FEBRUARY 6th:

We went walking up a mountain with the confused insurance company's sports club. Not so strange you might think, as that is what sports clubs are supposed to do with mountains. But, wait a minute – in January! What about the snow? There was a good half-metre or more of snow in places, but we were still able to walk thanks to snow shoes, those things that look like tennis racquets, strapped to our walking shoes. I was disappointed to find that they weren't tennis-racquet shaped, but roughly oval and are not the easiest things to walk up a mountain on. The walk was very strenuous, but it was probably better than walking in shoes alone. The organiser of the tour rented the snow shoes from the Swiss Army's snow shoe and tennis club.

FEBRUARY 9th:

It is fourteen months since the Swiss voted 'no thanks' to proposals to join the European Union. Later, Euro-fans were appeased by the Swiss then voting 'yes' to NEAT – the massive new rail tunnels project through the Alps. NEAT will relieve road congestion, but has been seen by some as merely an expensive present to the EU as it will allow EU member states to get their goods and holiday-makers through the Alps faster.

Now Euro-fans have been dealt a blow by a vote to approve, by a small margin, the *Alpeninitiative*. This has nothing to do with Mr Kellogg's breakfast cereal, but the protection of the Alps, in particular the Swiss ones. The initiative calls for all goods vehicles travelling from border to border through Switzerland and crossing the Alps to be 'piggybacked' on special trains.

Carrying lorries by train has already been done for some years, but it is not used much and the fear is that when the new tunnels are built under the NEAT scheme, 'piggybacking' will be under-utilised. This new initiative, which comes into force in ten years' time, will mean lorries are forced to go on the trains. There are alternatives, like driving through Austria or France.

The French-speaking Swiss voted against it, and well they might, as lorries don't need to come through their side of the fried-potato ditch to cross the Alps. In accepting the *Alpeninitiative*, Switzerland is breaking its transit agreements with the EU and opponents of the scheme claim it was a vote against the European Union. The Swiss now fear retaliation from the EU. But it's fair; I'm sure the Swiss would be very happy to send their lorries by train through all EU member countries which have Alps. It's time for the Swiss to stop worrying and get down to digging those tunnels.

The Swiss won't really dig the tunnels themselves, of course. They will pay someone else to get their hands dirty, like some of the 155,000 foreigners who come over the borders every day to work. Known as *Grenzgänger* (border crossers) these workers represent about 5% of the Swiss workforce. 32,000 come each day from Germany, 9,000 from Austria, 38,000 from Italy and the most, 76,000, from France.

What brings these hoards over the borders in such a large daily migration? The crinkly stuff – Swiss francs. On average, *Grenzgänger* earn double the money they would doing the equivalent job in their own countries. Are there any Swiss who cross the borders to work in neighbouring countries? Well, we do know one. Our sister-in-law, Angela, wife of Andreas and a psychiatrist. She pops over to Germany once a week to shrink a few heads and pick up cheap meat, cream and butter.

MARCH 21st:

The Swiss continue to pour out their soul over the *Alpeninitiative*, whereby in ten years lorries in transit through Switzerland must be sent by rail. They feel that the rest of Europe is now lined up against them and will take retaliatory action.

I try to explain whenever I can that, as far as Britain is concerned at least, no one has any idea what Switzerland is up to and many British do not even know where Switzerland is, and they certainly don't care about the *Alpeninitiative*. I am sure Britain's attempts to change, for example, the EU voting arrangements were far more controversial than anything Switzerland could dream up.

APRIL 1st:

You will recall the official *Züri-Sacks* which cost far more than normal plastic rubbish-bags. I forecast that the price of these would go up, since it was actually cheaper for us than the previous system. I was right. Beginning next year, the cost of official bags will be doubled as will the fine for putting out rubbish in an unofficial bag.

Meanwhile the people of the town of Zurich have been so careful with what they throw out that those in charge of the town's incinerator, which generates electricity, have had to import rubbish from all over the canton and beyond to keep generating power.

APRIL 16th:

The Swiss equivalent of the annual British Ministry of Transport Test for cars, or MOT, the *MFK* (*Motorfahrzeugkontrolle*) is a three-yearly event and by all accounts a strict affair. My car was due for this test in February, but as no one will buy a used car without one, the demand for tests is high from people selling secondhand cars. The authorities are currently running a few months behind schedule. To add to the horror of it all, I have now been sent a 'forewarning' in the post just to get me in the mood for it. The notice advises that my car will be called in for testing in two to four months' time. My knees are already knocking.

On the subject of cars, our neighbours' car has been stolen. A dull and aging VW Golf. They informed the police who were of the opinion that the car was well on its way to the former eastern block, where there is a big demand for dull and aging Golfs.

The same day I read a feature in THE TIMES advising that car theft is now rampant in the UK where 7.7% of cars are stolen. Switzerland came bottom of the list with car thefts running at 0.0%. It just goes to show that you can't believe everything that you read in the papers.

APRIL 18th:

Today was Zurich's odd afternoon holiday, *Sächsilüüte* – six o'clock ringing. This year we braved cold winds and grey skies to go and see the procession and the burning of the snowman for ourselves, instead of watching it on TV. Last year the snowman, or *Böög*, fell off the top of the huge bonfire before a single flame had reached him. We found what looked like a good position forty-five minutes before the bonfire was lit. There were about three rows of people between us and the square where the snowman is burnt. After his ignominy last time, the snowman wore a crash helmet and had plasters on is face from his fall.

After our wait, were we rewarded with a good view of the festivities? No such luck. Two minutes before the fire was lit a man at the front with three children decided they had sat long enough on the wall that surrounds the square and promptly stood his three kids on it. This completely blocked our view and that of the people near us. Despite our protests, in stoic Swiss style he proffered the explanation that they had waited for three hours and they were going to stand on the wall whatever anyone else thought of it. In sarcastic desperation Regula handed the man our video camera saying that if his children were going to ruin our view, could he at least video it for us. He refused that too.

We fought our way further back from the square where we were able to see the flaming snowman fall over again before his head had blown off as the bonfire collasped. They clearly don't build fires like they used to.

APRIL 20th:

Our neighbours have been reunited with their car. It was not bumping along the roads of Eastern Europe, but neatly parked and locked a couple of streets away from where they left it. Or rather, where they think they left it. At least this would comply with THE TIMES' Swiss car-theft figure of 0.0%.

Still on a four-wheeled theme, here's a little conversation stopper from the not-many-people-know-that department: every two thousandth car in Switzerland is a Ferrarri. That's the highest level of ownership of Ferrarris in the world.

APRIL 22nd – MAY 6th:

Time for another visit to the 'old country'. We flew over with Swissair. All non-EU nationals, which includes the Swiss, must complete a landing card to hand in at British immigration. The stewardess came round during the flight to London asking everyone whether or not they had an "English passport." There is no such thing. When she asked me, like a clever-dickie I said "no." Before I could point out to her that it should be a British or UK passport, she had given me a landing card and had moved on to the row behind.

I always say that I don't see a big difference between England and Switzerland when I go back, and this still holds true. The more so with the arrival in the UK of cycle lanes. Now Britain is cursed with automatic radar cameras to nab speeding motorists and those who jump red lights. Zurich council would be proud of some of Bournemouth's roads with their new suspension-punishing force of sleeping policemen. Bournemouth council still have to learn that these should be constructed from expensive rare marble not cheap asphalt-covered concrete, but otherwise they would fit perfectly into any Swiss street.

Regula flew back earlier via Gatwick. At the check-in desk she was selected for a special security scrutiny. I am all for anything that makes air travel safer. But imagine my surprise when the ground hostess handed Regula her case back and asked if she would take it herself to the special security office some fifty metres down the hall. I could not believe it and I queried this with the two security officers as they X-rayed her bag very carefully. If we were carrying a bomb, I reasoned, we wouldn't bring it round to their office for them to find in our luggage. They replied that this is what they were told to do by the airport authority and theirs was not to reason why. I suppose the security check works to the extent that the occasional would-be bomber is tipped off and has to go home and try again another day.

My own return journey via Heathrow meant an early start and I was there well before 6.30 am. I had an uncomfortable wait in the departure lounge where

I simply wanted to read my newspaper, but idiots insisted on talking on mobile phones all around me. Apparently it is not only important for other people to know that you have one of these devices, this has to be re-enforced by shouting loudly into the apparatus. I had to move away twice to read in peace.

The conversations they conducted at full volume were all broadly the same and went along the lines:

"Oh, sorry to wake you. Yeh, I'm in the departure lounge at Heathrow." A couple of questions were posed to the caller, which in each case was answered with "Yes... Yes... Don't be like that." And finally, "Bye." The questions could well have been 'Don't you know what time it is?' Followed by: 'You'd have been better off buying a watch instead of that wretched phone.' And finally 'The sooner your batteries run down the better, in fact please leave that phone of yours wherever it is you're going.'

MAY 7th

Back in Switzerland I have a moment to reflect on modern life in both countries. Britain is still smarting from years of recession, the depth of which is not really comprehensible to most Swiss.

The three million Britons who are out of a job represent 11% unemployment. This is over double the Swiss level. But it does not tell the full story. Many of those still working in Britain are on short contracts with little security. Others have been forced into self-employment when their long-standing contracts of employment were torn up. There is no longer such a thing as a secure job. I asked a friend who is a fireman if business was still good. He replied that, although fires still burned, in order to save money the number of fireman to put them out had been cut.

Unemployment stalks all walks of British life. All forms of business and commerce, as well as public services, have been squeezed by lack of money beyond what was once thought to be normal limits. Even in the 'prosperous' south of England it is possible to walk through shopping streets where only one shop in three remains in business.

Our house in England, that we have not put up for sale in the hope of an improvement in the market, reflects this general economic malaise. Houses have been losing about 10% of their value every year for the last five years. And we are some of the lucky ones because there are now 1.5 million British households in 'negative equity'. This is a new expression born in the recession. It means that 1.5 million houses are now worth less than the mortgage that was raised to buy them. But, far from throwing themselves from the nearest cliff, the British are philosophical, living in hope of an improvement before too long and there seems no talk of a revolution.

Poor economic prospects aside, the British have always understood any-one who leaves their country to live elsewhere. Whereas the Swiss are more happy to stay in their land and always seem a little surprised that anyone from England should actually prefer living in Switzerland. Reflecting their negative nature, the Swiss say more in astonishment than as a question: "Do you **like** living here?" Furthermore I have been asked more often, not what I like, but what I do **not** like about Switzerland. This is much better than the favourite British question to foreigners: "How long are you here for and when do you go back?"

Compared to the UK, life is very comfortable in Switzerland. There are more things I like in Switzerland than dislike, that is why I continue to live here. However, the Swiss seem more interested in my dislikes.

So, it's cards-on-the-table-time. Here are my dislikes:

- smoking and smoking-associated complaints, such as loud coughing and excessive spitting in public.
- dogs in restaurants – strictly forbidden in animal-loving Britain, but in Switzerland it is not uncommon to come across somebody's hound under your table. This applies not only to mountain restaurants, but to fashionable and expensive Zurich establishments.
- cycling on the pavement – Swiss cyclists are very well provided for in comparison to the UK, but they and moped riders seem to insist on riding where pedestrians walk. It's dangerous and against the law, but they do it whenever possible.

However, there is one pet hate that stands out above all others: how the Swiss use what I can best describe as their personal space. Like all British tourists, I have long been perturbed by foreigners who are incapable of forming anything remotely resembling a half-decent queue. The Swiss inability to queue is only the tip of the iceberg. In plain English: they are forever getting in the way!

When Swiss friends meet in the street, they become oblivious to the rest of the world. With dogs or children in pushchairs or wheeled shopping-bags, the pavement is soon blocked. One often has difficulty in getting off a Zurich tram because when the automatic doors open, there is a human wall of would-be passengers all eager to board. It is obvious they cannot get on the tram until those who are getting off, have got off. But this does not seem to occur to them and they are oddly puzzled that people getting off need to push their way past them.

Having commuted into London for a number of years, I understand the importance of standing to one side on escalators. When you are not in a hurry, standing to one side lets those who are get past. In Zurich, where more people are in more of a rush than in most places in the world, they never stand to one side. The Zurchers form, as if by intention, a snake-pattern on escalators, making passing an impossibility.

This inability to understand the effect of their actions on others is demonstrated by the car driver and pavement parking. According to my Swiss highway code, titled "Handbook of Swiss Traffic Regulations" and translated into perfect English, rule number 94 states "Parking on the pavement is prohibited." (There are a few places where the pavement is marked with yellow paint as authorised parking places.) On the move, Swiss motorists are highly disciplined, but when they park they become absolute cowboys. It is not uncommon for pedestrians to find their way blocked by cars parked, not only illegally, but without the slightest thought for anyone else.

When the tram is full and passengers are standing, you will find people sitting on the aisle seats, preventing anyone else using the window seats. Like motorists, tram passengers appear to be blissfully unaware of others around them and the effect they have on them.

To understand this mysterious attitude of the Swiss, I first had to discover why we British are different. Regula drew my attention to an expression that she came across many years ago while shopping in England: 'let the lady pass'. Up and down the high streets of the British Isles, shops and supermarkets ring to the sound of anxious mothers instilling manners into their receptive preschool infants with this most British of expressions.

From the age when they can walk, the British are trained to give way to others. In later life they are unable to shake off this Pavlovian reflex to 'let the lady pass'. We poor British can be seen giving way, opening doors and queuing for the rest of our days. The Swiss equivalent of 'let the lady pass' does not exist. This is clear from the 'queue' at ski lifts to the occupying of seats on public transport. Swiss children walk along the pavement five abreast, proving that there is another generation coming along who have not the slightest idea that the lady, or anyone else, wants to pass. They seem to think that they are the only people in the world. But I am beginning to wonder if this could be that elusive Holy Grail of Swiss success.

The Swiss are obviously doing something right. If you measure success by a country's output (gross national product) per citizen, then Switzerland is unbeatable – 41% ahead of their prosperous German neighbours, 42% ahead of Japan, 57% ahead of the USA and more than double that of the United Kingdom. Switzerland has found the elixir of economic growth without high inflation. Its citizens earn amongst the highest wages in the world and pay low taxes.

As a small landlocked country with difficult terrain and no natural mineral resources to speak of, Switzerland should be labouring under a heavy disadvantage in the economic glow of the late twentieth century. There is tourism, but Britain has nearly twice as many tourists a year as Switzerland. Add to Switzerland's disadvantages the lack of heavy industry, the confusion and conflict of uniting the speakers of four languages and four cultures and Switzerland should have been written off years ago. Without guaranteed colonial markets abroad and a home market smaller than London, not a member of the European Union, not even a member of the United Nations, Switzerland should be a westerly Albania and yet it is a mountainous Dallas.

The Swiss behave as if they are unable to see over the mountain into the next valley and so think they are the only people on this earth. This has bred a lonely fear in Swiss hearts that drives them to work hard. It makes them prepare for every eventuality. It makes them save and worry, and save a bit more, and then worry some more. I have lost count of the times I have been told by the Swiss that their prosperity is coming to an end and their country is on the brink of collapse. It would be no surprise to learn that they had been saying that for the last seven hundred years or so.

May 12th – 15th:

Our pals Mark and Maggie came over for a few days' break. The first time they visited us, I had covered less than 15 kilometres in our new car when I was unfairly photographed doing 68kph in a 50 zone. Since then I have been a veritable angel behind the wheel. Until, that is, this visit. No sooner had they gone than I received a Sfr 40 (£18) fine from the police in one of the cantons we went through with them. Apparently I was doing 112kph in a 100 zone and was photographed by infrared camera, no flashes this time.

Mark and Maggie made me realise that I have got so used to the odd mix of English and Swiss-German Regula and I use that I don't notice it anymore.

Regula bought some rabbit to cook one evening and she was very pleased to find that rabbit was on special offer, which the Swiss call *Aktion*. When Regula announced "the rabbits were all *Aktion* in Migros", I thought nothing of it, but Mark imagined the rabbits were alive, had escaped and were bouncing round the store.

If my English is going, then this must be the end.

EPILOGUE

Much has been written about adapting to a new society and the culture shock that can follow. I am just one of a long line of people who changed their land, starting with Adam and Eve leaving Eden. My adaptation to Swiss society has been helped by being able to escape – literally, with trips to England, and metaphorically by playing the tourist. But I cannot remain an eternal spectator; if I had come to Zurich aged four, I would have forgotten my English long ago. Even at fourteen Swiss-German would be stronger than English by now. But at forty things take a little longer. Now, half way through my fifth year in Switzerland I admit that I am considering getting to grips with Swiss-German. I'm finding my Swiss role!

What then of the Perpetual Tourist? (I think it is finally time for capitals.) To remain a kind of eternal holiday-maker in a land where the enthusiasm for work remains high is unrealistic and even a dangerous delusion. I have some difficulty in admitting it, but the Perpetual Tourist is not so perpetual, he represents a phase in my adaption to living in Switzerland. I shall not easily say goodbye to the Perpetual Tourist and I feel sure that he will be called upon in the future to show me the way when the Swiss going gets tough.

There will be times when I need to view the world through sunglasses and be a tourist again. Like an American who was spotted in a Zurich car park wrestling with a map of Switzerland on the bonnet of his rented car. In a rich Texan accent, he asked a passing Swiss if she knew the way to the Matterhorn. He was pointed in the right direction but warned that it would take at least five hours to get there. Undaunted, the tourist folded his map and was last seen driving off in the direction of the Matterhorn. This was related to me as an amusing encounter of the tourist kind. The Swiss often laugh at such antics from their tourists.

If, like me, you find nothing too unusual about a day trip to the Matterhorn, then you are good tourist material. When life starts to get you down, try looking at the world with the surprise and joy that comes from being a tourist at heart. Never pondering too long. Certainly not worrying. Noticing the nice things and missing the nasty. Asking naïve questions and being content with naïve answers. Always discovering the new and the novel. Waking each day to a new adventure. Prepared to be spontaneous and unprepared to plan. Why not put on the sunglasses of life and try being a Perpetual Tourist too?

About Bergli Books:

Bergli Books Ltd. publishes, promotes and distributes books in English on intercultural issues of particular interest to Europeans. We also encourage people who live and work outside their country or language of origin to write about their intercultural adaptation and their experiences in coping with cultural differences.

Bergli Books Ltd. is a private corporation, without religious or political affiliations. It is not supported by any industry or institution. Your help in spreading the word about these intercultural books is appreciated.

All manuscripts are welcome but must be accompanied by an International Reply Coupon or a Swiss stamped, self-addressed envelope or they cannot be returned. Bergli Books Ltd. cannot be held responsible for unsolicited manuscripts.

Ticking Along with the Swiss

Collected and edited by Dianne Dicks

A collection of thirty stories from English-speaking writers, translators, teachers and journalists who have been steadily 'ticking along with the Swiss' for many years. Their stories cover topics of interest to anyone associated with the Swiss or Switzerland.

These personal experiences are written in various styles ranging from playful nonsense to dead seriousness, for example:

- a psychiatrist writes about culture shock,
- an Afro-American tells about his experiences as a teenager living with the Swiss,
- amusing accounts of communication difficulties and challenges
- an entertaining A to Z giving important aspects of living with the Swiss and their habits
- evaluations about sisterhood and
- how to become a Swiss soldier without knowing a Swiss language.

This is not a book of etiquette for 'foreigners' living in Switzerland, it simply shows how to live here without losing one's identity. Swiss people will enjoy looking at themselves from a new perspective.

New revised edition by Bergli Books Ltd. available autumn 1994. ISBN 3-9520002-4-8

Ticking Along Too

Stories about Switzerland

Collected and edited by Dianne Dicks

How do foreigners get along with the Swiss?

What about Swiss humor?

Are Swiss dead on time?

Was Switzerland always so clean?

Have you got a Swiss mother-in-law?

Do you need to make your Swiss neighbors smile?

Fifty humorous, thought-provoking and informative personal experiences of authors of nine nationalities about living in Switzerland. These stories are a mix of social commentary, warm admiration tempered by criticism, observations of national or local character traits.

You'll get perspectives from all regions of Switzerland, from its cities, countryside, mountains, homes, offices and even from its ladies rooms. Whether you've just arrived in Switzerland, lived here many years or always dreamed of living here, this collection will give you lots to laugh and think about, especially if you're Swiss. ISBN 3-9520002-1-3

Cupid's Wild Arrows;

intercultural romance and its consequences

Collected and edited by Dianne Dicks

Is your partner from another culture, country, language, race or religion?

Are intercultural marriages really more difficult?

Do they have some advantages?

What conflicts can be expected?

What happens to children of bi-cultural marriages?

How can you keep your own sense of identity?

A collection of personal experiences from 55 authors of many different nationalities whose love relationships required crossing cultural frontiers. Some of these couples came from opposite sides of the world, some grew up within 100 miles of each other. But all of these relationships demand that at least one partner adapts to a new culture.

Topics covered: Beyond Frontiers, Thresholds, Children, Food, Language, Coping with Differences, Coping with Crisis, Family Influences, Identities, Advice from the Clever and the Wise.

Whether she comes from China, he from Lebanon, whether they live in Denmark or Samoa, whether one of them has to learn to speak Bimoba or how to say 'no' in English, these couples go through all the trials of a 'normal' romance and more.
ISBN 3-9520002-2-1

Dear Reader,

Your opinion can help us. We would like to know what you think of the book you have in your hands.

Where did you learn about this book?

Had you heard about Bergli Books before reading this book?

What did you enjoy about this book?

Any criticism?

Would you like to receive more information about the books we publish and distribute? If so, please give us your name and address:

Name:
Address:
City/Country

Cut out page, fold here, staple and mail to:

Bergli Books Ltd.
CH-6353 Weggis
Switzerland